CHICKEN SOUP
FOR THE
COUNTRY SOUL

CHICKEN SOUP FOR THE COUNTRY SOUL

Stories Served Up Country-Style and Straight from the Heart

Jack Canfield
Mark Victor Hansen
Ron Camacho

Health Communications, Inc.
Deerfield Beach, Florida
www.chickensoup.com

We would like to acknowledge the following publishers and individuals for permission to reprint the following material. (Note: The stories that were penned anonymously, that are public domain or were written by Jack Canfield, Mark Victor Hansen or Ron Camacho are not included in this listing.)

Giving. Reprinted by permission of Randy Travis. All rights reserved.

Love Goes a Long Way, Mama Sang a Song and *Just What the Doctor Ordered.* Reprinted by permission of Whisperin' Bill Anderson. ©1998 Whisperin' Bill Anderson.

Sir . . . My Waiting Room Angel. Reprinted by permission of Carla M. Fulcher. ©1998 Carla M. Fulcher.

Bottom Dollar. Reprinted by permission of Robert J. Duncan and the June 1995 *Reader's Digest.* ©1995 Robert J. Duncan.

The Man in Black. Reprinted by permission of Richard Tripp. ©1998 Richard Tripp.

O Holy Night. Reprinted by permission of Jean Calvert. ©1998 Jean Calvert.

(Continued on page 252)

ISBN 1-55874-563-7

Publisher: Health Communications, Inc.
          3201 S.W. 15th Street
          Deerfield Beach, FL 33442-8190

Cover design by Andrea Perrine Brower

This book is dedicated with love
and appreciation to the performers of
The Grand Ole Opry and to ALL the people
who have enriched our lives by singing, performing
and working toward the evolution of country music.
We have been lifted out of loneliness, reminded
of our core American values, heartbroken
and healed, and inspired to go for greatness
by your songs and your lives.

The last two years have seen the
passing of far too many legendary personalities.
Chicken Soup for the Country Soul would like to remember:
Owen Bradley, Sarah Ophelia "Minnie Pearl" Cannon,
Floyd Cramer, Grandpa Jones, Bill Monroe,
Patsy Montana, Carl Perkins, David "Skull" Schulman,
Chuck Seals, Cliffie Stone, Justin Tubb,
Tammy Wynette and Faron Young.
Your memories will live in our hearts forever.

This book is dedicated to country life
and the tradition that has come to
be known as country music.

Country music is America. It started here, it's ours. It isn't something that we learned from some other nation; it isn't something we inherited, and so it's as native as anything we can find. It comes from the heart of America. It talks about family. It talks about religion, the faith of God that is so important to our country, and particularly, to our family life; and, as we all know, country music radiates of this nation's patriotism; it's good for Americans to hear it. We come away better for having heard it.

Richard M. Nixon
At the Reopening of the Grand Ole Opry

Contents

2. ON FAMILY

3. THE POWER OF FAITH

4. LIVING THE DREAM

5. OVERCOMING OBSTACLES AND HARDSHIPS

6. THE POWER OF A SONG

Acknowledgments

First a huge thank-you to our families!

To Jack's wife, Georgia, and his son, Christopher, who in the midst of the pressure-filled weeks it takes to finish a book like this, constantly remind him to slow down, smell the roses, and listen to some music. To Jack's parents, who instilled in him a love of music and helped him buy his first guitar.

To Mark's wife, Patty, who constantly supports his writing and editing work, and to his daughters, Elisabeth and Melanie, who share their dad with his work.

To Ron's beloved wife, Ellen, and precious daughter, Angelique, for their constant support and sacrifice. Through lengthy absences and heavy workloads their constant renewing energy kept him going and made this whole adventure worth it. To Ron's mother, Angela Camacho, for her clairvoyant monetary donations and endless faith in Ron's abilities.

We also wish to acknowledge the following people:

Our dear friend and Ron's partner, Julie Barnes, who introduced Ron to Mark and Jack and has been working alongside us for three years. Your personal and professional support made it possible for us to get through the many trials we faced along the way. Your love and support are inexpressibly dear to us. And your patience and inexhaustible enthusiasm are deeply appreciated. To Julie's mother, Judy Barnes, for her constant energies in both problem solving and endless spiritual support.

Heather McNamara, our senior editor, who was the project coordinator for this book. She was instrumental at every stage—compiling, editing, sequencing, choosing quotes and cartoons, and keeping the whole thing on track in the midst of constant chaos.

Nancy Mitchell, who managed to continually find the gold nuggets among the thousands of stories we sifted through, and found cartoons and quotes. We also thank her for her incredible effectiveness and perseverance in getting all the permissions we needed.

Patty Aubery, who contributed immensely during the final few weeks with the final selection of stories, editing and overseeing every aspect of the production, and still managing the day-to-day activities of the staff of The Canfield Group and Self-Esteem Seminars—all while being pregnant! Welcome Chandler Scott!

Kimberly Kirberger, for being the managing editor of this project in its early stages and for continuing to show faith in this endeavor when things seemed to be slowing to a halt. Through her caring, consoling and hard work we were able to redirect and continue our efforts. Thanks for hanging in there with us through the tough times.

Rochelle Pennington, for selecting many of the quotes we use throughout this book.

Veronica Romero, Teresa Esparza, Lisa Williams, Laurie Hartman, Ro Miller and Robin Yerian, for holding down the fort while the rest of us wrote and edited.

Leslie Forbes, for providing any assistance we needed to complete this project, especially the wonderful aid in obtaining permissions that she gave Nancy.

Preshias Tomes and Jeanne Cecil in the American

Entertainment Concepts office, for keeping Ron sane and in one piece during the worst of it.

Sharon Linnéa, Erica Orloff, Donna Peerce and, especially, chief storyteller Don Dible, for their excellent and timely help with editing some of the stories in this book—often with little advance warning.

Anna Kansen at *Guideposts*, who once again came through at the last minute to help us identify several outstanding stories which we have used.

Mark and Chrissy Donnelly, who helped us with some of the final stories.

Porter Wagoner, for calling the session that brought us the incredible song "In the Shade of the Family Tree"—which we have included on the CD in this book—and to Porter and the 112 Opry stars and country legends who performed on the record. Special thanks to Capitol Records for Garth Brooks; MCA Records for Vince Gill, Trisha Yearwood and Marty Stuart; Sony Records for Patty Loveless and Joe Diffie; RS Entertainment for Ricky Skaggs; Capri Chambliss, Porter's assistant, for assisting us in all aspects of the CD project and permissions.

Also to our personal friend Gwendolyn Kay Skipper, an artist as well as a former vocalist with Ronnie Milsap, for giving us the first drawings of this book cover. Your smiles and loving support helped us begin this journey. You left this world too soon. We miss you.

Stormy Warren of Jim Owens and Associates, for helping us to get the first word out about this project through the *TNN News* and for helping us get on *Crook and Chase*. To Lorianne Crook and Charlie Chase, for having us on their show.

Teresa George of the Country Music Association, for believing in us early on and for helping us get the word out through *CMA Close Up*.

Phyllis Hill of TNN, and Ronnie Pugh and Kent

Henderson of the Country Music Foundation's library, for opening their archives to us and for all the assistance and information they provided us when we needed it the most.

Kathy Gangwich, Bruce Burch and Vernell Hackett, for giving us their time and connections as well as their friendship. Also thanks to Vernell for assisting us with some of the editing.

Bob Whittaker and Jerry Strobel, stage managers of the Grand Ole Opry, for their continuous hospitality.

Ron's brother in Christ, Billy Walker—the "Tall Texan"— who was a true friend and so graciously introduced Ron to all the people at the Opry.

Bill Anderson, Jan Howard, Skeeter Davis, Johnny Counterfeit, Buck White, Stonewall Jackson, Little Jimmy Dickens, Joe Diffie, Vince Gill, and the whole Opry cast, for their constant smiles, concern and support.

Loudilla, Loretta and Kay Johnson of the International Fan Club Organization, for helping us solicit stories from all of their wonderful fan clubs. With their constant e-mails, faxes and letters we were able to reach out to the fans, whose amazing energy, enthusiasm and loyalty to their favorite artists continually impressed us.

Mike Smith at The Nashville Scene, who helped us solicit stories from local artists, songwriters and fans.

Joe Moscheo and Kathy Kinsch at the First Union Bank, who helped Ron expand his activities at American Entertainment Concepts during this crucial time.

Martin Clayton, Donna Priesmeyer and Kate Haggerty at Interactive Media and CBS Cable, who helped us make literary history. Through their Web site at country.com, we were able, for the first time in history, to involve thousands of country music fans in helping us decide the final content of this book by evaluating and commenting on over fifty stories.

Larry and Susan Blankenship, for designing our

AMENTCO Web site, which later became the model for country.com and IFCO.com.

Barbara "Bobbi" Smith, Carolyn Halloran, Rita LeFevre and Karla Adam, who helped us conduct valuable research for the book.

Jonnie Barnett and Rory Lee, the winners of the story-writing contest we sponsored during the final phases of the project, whose story, "The Chain of Love," appears in this book.

And last, but not least, Jimmy Lowe, former drummer of the Pirates of the Mississippi, and his wife, Cindy, and also Tess Blyveis and her children, Nathan and Emily, for providing a home with hugs and love for Ron's first year in Nashville.

Thank you to the following people for taking the time to read and respond in the most complimentary and supportive fashion: Fred Angelis, Barbara Astrowsky, Patty Aubery, Judy Barnes, Christine Belleris, Samantha Berry, Emily, Nathan and Tess Blyveis, Terry Brown, Diana Chapman, Tom Corley, Robin Davis, Ron Delpier, Matthew Diener, Lisa Drucker, Thales Finchum, Randee Goldsmith, Melissa Goodson, Sherry Grimes, Nancy Richard Guilford, Vernell Hackett, Allison Janse, Tom Krause, Sharon Little, Donna Loesch, Inga Mahoney, Paige Manual, Heather McNamara, Susan Mendes, Linda Mitchell, Nancy Mitchell, Tomas Nani, Lance Nelson, Ron Nielson, Cindy Palajac, Kesha Pope, Dave Potter, April Robbings, Frank Saulino, Barbie and Bobbie Smith, Caroline Strickland, Jaltel Thomas, Peter Vegso, Debi Way, Rebecca Whitney, Martha Wigglesworth, and Maureen Wilcinsky.

Neil Pond, senior entertainment editor, *Country America Magazine*; Martin Clayton, vice president and general manager, *Interactive Media, CBS Cable*, country.com; Mark Edwards, operations manager, *Country Coast-to-Coast*, ABC

Radio Networks; Bob Cannon, editor in chief, *New Country Magazine*; Linda Fuller, senior producer, *SJS Entertainment*; Paula Ghergia, entertainment editor, *The Inside Connection*, Premier Motor Music Networking Company; Mike Greenblatt, editor, *Modern Screen's Country Music Magazine*; Vernell Hackett, editor, *American Songwriter Magazine*; Jackie Jarosz, editor, *Teen Country Magazine*; Loudilla Johnson, president and cofounder, International Fan Club Organization; Dick McVey, Nashville senior news editor, *Performance Magazine*; Erin Morris and Jim Della Croce, *The Press Office*; Ray Pilszak, director of national sales, *Amusement Business*; Jon Rawl, *Country Music Journalist*; Lindsey Rawl, segment producer, *Crook and Chase*; Al Wyntor, host, *NASCAR Country* and *On-Line to Music Row*; Richard McVey II, managing editor, *Music City News*.

All the other *Chicken Soup for the Soul* coauthors—current, past and future—for sharing abundantly of their resources and themselves in an incredible spirit of TEAM (Together Each Achieves More).

And to all the people at Health Communications, Inc.—our publisher—thanks a million! You can't believe how much goodness you shed upon our lives. We especially wish to thank:

Peter Vegso and Gary Seidler, for believing in this book from the moment it was proposed, supporting it, and skillfully helping us get it into the hands of millions of readers.

Christine Belleris, Matthew Diener, Allison Janse and Lisa Drucker, our editors at Health Communications, Inc., who skillfully take our work to the highest level possible before it is published.

Randee Goldsmith, the *Chicken Soup for the Soul* product manager at Health Communications, Inc., who is always there to support us and give us words of encouragement along the way.

Kim Weiss, Larry Getlen and Ronnie O'Brien, our

incredibly creative and effective publicists, who continue to help us keep our books on the bestsellers lists.

Claude Choquette, who manages year after year to get each of our books translated into over twenty languages around the world.

John and Shannon Tullius, John Saul, Mike Sacks, Bud Gardner, Dan Poynter, Bryce Courtney, Terry Brooks and all our other friends at the Maui Writers Conference and Retreat who inspire and encourage us every year.

We also wish to thank the over five hundred people who took the time to submit stories, poems and other pieces for consideration. You all know who you are. Without you this book could never have happened. While most of the stories submitted were wonderful, we were only able to include the stories you find here. The decisions were often agonizing. We hope in each case we have done what is best for the book.

Because of the immensity of this project, we may have left out names of some people who have helped us along the way. If so, we are sorry. Please know that we really do appreciate all of you.

We are truly grateful for the many hands and hearts that have made this book possible. We love and appreciate you all!

Introduction

Country music springs from the heart of America.

Tex Ritter

A song ain't nothin' in the world but a story just wrote with music to it.

Hank Williams Sr.

Three years ago Ron Camacho approached us with the idea of our compiling a book of *Chicken Soup* stories by and about country music artists. Because the *Chicken Soup for the Soul* books had been gathering and presenting stories from the heart of America for the past five years and country music had been doing the same thing through songs for over seventy, it was natural for the two to come together in a book of heartwarming stories to nurture the souls of country music fans and anyone else interested in the love, wit and wisdom that emanate from the world of country music.

With former tour manager Ron acting as the point man, we took off on a venture that would profoundly change our lives—especially Ron's. After a few months, it was clear we needed to go where the music and the artists

were. Ron actually relocated from Southern California to
Nashville—which we visited often—and began meeting
with artists and their managers. We all received a warm
welcome as people were excited about the project. Artists,
managers, agents, songwriters, deejays, journalists and
people at the record labels and the Country Music
Association all opened their office doors and their hearts
to us.

Then it was off to Lukenbach, Texas, for Willie Nelson's
Fourth of July Party and back to Nashville—where Ron
now resides—for Fan Fair, with lots of stops in between.
Along the way, we had the pleasure of making the
acquaintance of some of the warmest people we have ever
met—entertainers, writers, sound technicians, cowboy
poets, street prophets, pastors, and, most important,
country music fans. Everywhere we went, we were
treated with down-home cooking and neighborly hospitality. Before we were done, we must have asked over a
thousand people to submit a story for the book.

Porter Wagoner and Billy Walker at the Grand Ole Opry
introduced Ron to everyone he needed to meet, and *Prime
Time Country* and *Crook and Chase* welcomed Mark on their
shows to put the word out to get stories. The people at
country.com—a new country Web site—allowed us to
post stories every week for evaluation and the *Nashville
Scene* and *Country Weekly* helped us sponsor a story-
writing contest to solicit even more stories.

> *I go through a thousand songs to find ten for a
> new record.*
>
> Conway Twitty

Similar to Conway Twitty, we have gone through over
five hundred stories to end up with the stories that

appear in this book. While the decisions were often painful, we hope we have created a final result as good as any double-platinum record you have ever purchased. What you are about to read is the best of the best.

In the same spirit of bringing together the best of the best, Porter Wagoner of the Grand Ole Opry invited 112 Opry stars and country entertainers to come together to record "In the Shade of the Family Tree" as a fund-raiser for the Opry Trust Fund. We are proud that we have been able to include this song in a CD in this book and that twenty cents for each book sold will be donated to the Opry Trust Fund.

We are very excited about this book and the accompanying CD, and we hope that you will have as much fun reading and listening to them as we have had compiling and editing them.

We'd Like to Hear from You

We would love to hear your reactions to the stories in this book. Please let us know which stories are your favorites and how they have affected you.

Also, please send us stories you would like to see published in *A 2nd Helping of Chicken Soup for the Country Soul.* You can send us stories you have written or ones that you have read and liked from somewhere else—a book, newsletter, newspaper or magazine. If we choose to publish a submission, we will pay you for an original story and credit you for submitting someone else's story.

Send your stories to:

Chicken Soup for the Country Soul
P.O. Box 30880 • Santa Barbara, CA 93130
fax: 805-563-2945
To send e-mail or visit our Web site:
www.chickensoup.com

1

ON LOVE
AND KINDNESS

Great people are able to do great kindnesses.

Miguel de Cervantes

Giving

"Love is a verb."

Anonymous

Giving love is doing,
and there's always more to do.
Share with those in need,
and it will all come back to you.
For when life on earth is over
and your time to go has come,
You won't be judged by what you have,
but by good deeds you've done.
So greet with open arms
every soul you run into,
'cause giving love is doing,
and there's always more to do.

Randy Travis

Love Goes a Long Way

Love received and love given comprise the best form of therapy.

Gordon Allport

I have received some wonderful fan mail over the years. I've received letters from couples who have fallen in love with my music, gotten married because of my music and raised their children on my music. I've had fans write and tell me of playing my music at weddings and on special wedding anniversaries. I've even been told of fans playing my hymns at a loved one's funeral.

There have been many tender, touching letters, but one in particular, I will never forget. It came from a young lady in Canada, and it took me back to a night in the late sixties when I had played a concert in her hometown.

I remember the night well. Jan Howard was touring with me, and we were booked into an ice hockey arena in eastern Ontario. Prior to the show, we sat backstage killing time in the dressing room when a man came by and asked if he might speak with us a moment. We said sure, and he walked in.

He sat down and softly told us about a young man from the town who, he said, had wanted to attend our concert more than just about anything in the world. All he had talked about for weeks was our coming to town, telling everyone how he was looking forward to seeing our show. But only a few days before we arrived, this young man was critically injured in a motorcycle accident. And he was lying cut, badly broken and only semi-conscious in a hospital bed on the other side of town. The prognosis for his survival was not good.

"I have a feeling," our visitor continued, directing his request toward me, "that if you and Jan would just take a minute of your time and go by the hospital to see this young man, it would be the best medicine anyone could possibly give him. He may not even recognize you, but he'll know you were there. I can't tell you how much he loves and admires both of you. If you'll just go say hi, I'll be glad to drive you over and I'll bring you back."

Fortunately, there were two shows set for that night with over an hour's intermission scheduled between the ending of the first show and the beginning of the second. Jan and I agreed we would go to the hospital between shows. "But we've got to come directly back," I cautioned. "We can't afford to be late." The man said he understood fully, and he told us he would be in his car with the motor running outside the stage door at the end of the first show.

I was surprised to find, when we arrived at the hospital, that the "young man" we had been told about was a big, strapping dude, well over six feet tall and probably weighing over two hundred pounds. His name was Arthur, and to my further surprise, he was married and the father of several children. I had expected, for some reason, an irresponsible teenager.

Arthur was hurt every bit as badly as our visitor had indicated. I remember seeing legs in casts, arms in casts, wires and tubes connected to virtually every part of his body. He was apparently receiving large doses of medication, and he appeared to be only partially awake.

Jan and I walked over to his bedside and told him who we were. We told him we were sorry he had gotten banged up so bad that he couldn't make it to our show. And we told him that we fully expected him to get well so that the next time we were up that way he could come to see us. We tried to keep everything on a light, positive note, but it wasn't easy. The young man was obviously very seriously injured. He could barely move his eyes to let us know that he was even aware we were in the room. I left his side feeling less than hopeful.

But God is still in the miracle business. The next contact I had with him was a letter from the family a few months later telling me that Arthur was improving. And the letter thanked me over and over again for having taken the time to come see him.

"You and Jan coming to the hospital gave him the will to live," the letter said. "He says he is going to get well enough to come see your show next time you're here. And we believe he will."

I was back in the area again about a year later, and I thought of Arthur and wondered how he was and how his recovery might be coming along. I didn't have to wait very long for my answer. When we pulled up to the arena, here came a big, husky guy in a motorized wheelchair grinning from ear to ear. He hugged my neck so hard he nearly broke me in two. All the family hugged me too, saying repeatedly that our visit to his hospital room was the medicine that saved his life.

The next time I saw Arthur, he was in the parking lot outside my office in Nashville. He had gotten well enough to drive and with the help of a special apparatus connected to the steering column of his car, he drove nearly a thousand miles to come see us at the Grand Ole Opry. He was truly a living miracle.

I stayed in touch with him and his family over the years. I saw him several more times, and he never failed to mention the visit Jan and I had paid him during the darkest moments of his life. And then I didn't see him or hear from anyone in the family for quite some time. One day I received a letter from his oldest daughter. It was very simple and to the point. She said simply that Arthur had become very ill and had died. She told me very few details. But she wrote one line that will stay with me forever:

"Thanks to you," she said, "I had a daddy for twenty years."

Whisperin' Bill Anderson

Sir . . . My Waiting Room Angel

The five-minute drive to the hospital seemed to take hours. I leaned against the passenger door of the car and tried to let the coolness of the window calm me. My mother had sent her friend to come get me. How like Mom to think of me driving to the hospital in my worried and frantic state—I had just gotten the news that my father had suffered a massive heart attack. Shock, worry, uncertainty and sheer terror all bombarded me without yield. I could not speak. I could not think. It was as if an unseen force controlled every part of me. I whispered prayers that I was not too late.

When we arrived at the hospital, I ran through the emergency room doors and back to the room where my father was stretched out on a table. My beautiful mother was collapsed in a heap in the middle of the floor, crying uncontrollably. She saw me and extended her arms for me, and then I heard it—the thin shrill cry of a flatline.

Doctors, nurses and orderlies filled the room barking orders in that medical language you see on television. I heard the crash of equipment being pushed through emergency room doors and a series of blips and bleeps. A metal tray haphazardly crashed to the floor somewhere behind me and I heard one brave, calm soul counting down numbers, "One-Two-Three-Four-Five-Breathe! One-Two-Three-Four-Five-Breathe! Clear." A volt of electricity ran through my father lying helplessly on the table and at that moment a part of me died inside.

After several minutes, a comforting series of bleeps began. His heart was beating on its own again. The next few hours were frightening. A team of emergency technicians was constantly monitoring his vital signs; however, his condition had improved quite a bit.

While asking a nurse to watch over my mother, I excused myself and found an empty waiting room. Like many people in the midst of a crisis, I had been keeping a tight rein on my emotions. Now, I chose a couch in the farthest corner and collapsed. The tears flowed uncontrollably, the sick and helpless feeling in my gut returned full force, and the experience began to take its toll. I prayed out loud for guidance from above to please not let my daddy die. I prayed for strength so I could be there for my mother—but I didn't know from where that strength could possibly come. I was frightened and felt very small and very alone. I worried that my father would die without truly knowing just how much I loved him. We had always been close, but how . . . how could words describe that kind of love? I buried my head in my hands and continued crying.

Softly, on my left shoulder, I felt a hand. Through tear-filled eyes I looked up and there he was. An elderly man with piercing eyes as blue as an autumn sky and a face of weathered leather. His once-powerful frame was now slightly bent and covered by a well-worn pair of overalls.

"It's okay, child. It's gonna be okay," his gruff, yet softened voice whispered to me. "You know you don't have to worry none 'bout your daddy knowing how you feel."

A puzzled look in my eyes beckoned him to continue as his strong hands pulled mine from my face and comforted me.

"Your daddy knows how much you love him, he always has, and no matter what happens, he will always be with you."

I had no idea how this stranger could have known what I was feeling inside, but this sweet man sat down beside me and gently put his arm around me, rocking me slowly back and forth. I spent an hour in this isolated waiting room with this comforting soul at my side, discussing prayers and memories of my father. He told me his wife was also in the critical care ward dying of cancer and was not expected to live but a few days. I expressed my sorrow for his soon-to-be loss and asked what I could do for him and his wife.

"What's to be will be. My wife and I have lived and loved each other a long, long time. Forever it seems. My loss is soothed by the comfort of eternal peace—your situation is much different. Hush now child, you rest, I will wake you if there is any news."

Weary and completely drained of energy, I soon drifted off to sleep being held by a stranger. A nurse accompanied my mother into the waiting room where I was resting and gently woke me.

"Your father has been moved to a critical care room. He is out of immediate danger; however, it will be a long night. We have arranged to have a couple of cots moved into the room so you may stay with him. He is a very lucky man." She quickly left the room to attend to other patients.

Mom sat down beside me and I quickly glanced around the room for my stranger. He was gone. I wanted to tell her what had happened, but she soon fell asleep, overwhelmed with exhaustion. She leaned her head on my shoulder and dozed as I held her close. Miraculously, I felt peace and strength I didn't know I had. I assumed it was from the utter calm of the stranger in the waiting room. I can't explain it, but when I looked in his blue eyes and he told me to rest and not worry, I had felt his calmness transfer to me.

Dad remained in the hospital for several weeks. I never left his side. My eyes glued to the monitors praying those bleeps did not stop. I slept in short intervals, frequenting the cafeteria for a shot of caffeine and occasionally I would see the man from the waiting room. Each time we bumped into each other, he would whisper with a twinkle in his eye, "He's doing better today isn't he?"

"Yes sir, he is. Thank you for sitting with me. How is your wife doing?" I questioned.

"Now, now child, I told you, an eternal peace is comfort. She has her days—some are good, some are bad."

"What room is she in? Perhaps I can bring the two of you some dinner later?" I asked eagerly wanting to repay the kindness.

"Ah, child, my memory is a lot older than my body is. I can't recall the room number, but I can always find my way to her. We'll be alright, you just take care of your daddy."

Over the next few weeks, Dad improved daily. I continued to bump into the kind gentleman. Unfortunately, I was always by myself because I wanted so badly to introduce him to my family. However, the opportunity never arose. I always looked forward to seeing him and even once wandered through the critical care ward peeking into rooms to see if perhaps I could find him. I wanted to do something nice for him, but I never found him.

The night before my father's release was the first good night's rest I had the entire time he was hospitalized. That night, the lumpy recliner, which had given me many backaches all the many nights before, felt exceptionally comfortable. I curled up in a blanket the nurse had given me and quickly fell asleep. Sometime after midnight, I awoke suddenly. My heart pounding, I studied the monitors above Dad's bed making sure they were working. I looked over at mom sleeping peacefully and realized I must have just been dreaming. I curled up into the blanket and just happened to glance over to the window. Through the half-closed blinds, I saw the blue-eyed old man. He raised one weathered finger to his lips, "Sssshh" and smiled. He waved and went on his way. I slept soundly the remainder of the evening.

The next day was exciting for me as I helped Mom pack Dad's belongings and loaded the car. After the nurse whisked Dad away in the wheelchair, I ran back to the room for one last look around making certain we did not leave anything behind. Then I found a nurse—I just had to thank my friend. He had sustained me through long weeks when I didn't think I could go on. Yet I always had. He always appeared when I needed him most.

"Nurse, an older man has been on this ward at his wife's side. You must have seen him wandering around. He's fairly tall, white-haired, deep blue eyes. And he's very sweet. I'd like to say good-bye to him."

"I'm sorry. That's not ringing a bell with me. Hold on. . . ." the nurse said. She went and got a supervisor, and I explained again how the old man had been a great source of comfort to me and I needed to say good-bye. They went over the list of patients, but not one older woman was listed on the critical care ward.

"We have several older men and a couple of car accident victims, but no women on this floor."

After asking around, no one could even recall seeing the old man. I was completely perplexed. Surely I hadn't imagined this man. He had to be in the hospital somewhere. But more questioning of nurses and orderlies drew a complete blank. Sadly, I realized I would have to leave without saying a proper good-bye.

Later that night, after Dad was settled at home, I reflected on the mysterious stranger. Maybe the old man himself was the answer to my prayers in that lonely waiting room. That elderly gentleman with those strong, weathered hands, the faded overalls and those deep, piercing blue eyes was a prayer answered for me. He helped me through one of the most difficult times in my life with his gentle voice and kind words. He brought me peace and hope at a time when I thought none could be found. Perhaps he was sent as my daddy's guardian angel. Or mine. My very own waiting room angel.

Carla M. Fulcher

Bottom Dollar

Cameron Mounger and I have been friends since we were teenagers. Both of us liked music, and several years after we left high school, Cam became a disc jockey.

Recently he told me the story about the day he was down to his last dollar. It was the day his luck—and his life—changed.

The story began in the early 1970s when Cam was an announcer and disc jockey at KYAL in McKinney, Texas, and attained celebrity status. He met many music stars, and he enjoyed flying to Nashville in the company plane with the station owner.

One night Cam was in Nashville for the final performance of the Grand Ole Opry at the Ryman Auditorium before it moved to Opryland U.S.A. "After the show, an acquaintance invited me backstage with all the Opry stars. I didn't have any paper for autographs, so I took out a dollar bill," Cam told me. "Before the night ended, I had virtually every Opry personality's autograph. I guarded that dollar bill and carried it with me always. I knew I would treasure it forever."

Then station KYAL was put up for sale, and many employees found themselves without a job. Cam landed part-time work at WBAP in Fort Worth and planned to hang on to this job long enough for a full-time position to open up.

The winter of 1976–77 was extremely cold. The heater in Cam's old Volkswagen emitted only a hint of warm air; the windshield defroster didn't work at all. Life was hard, and Cam was broke. With the help of a friend who worked at a local supermarket, he occasionally intercepted Dumpster-bound outdated TV dinners. "This kept my wife and me eating, but we still had no cash."

One morning as Cam left the radio station he saw a young man sitting in an old yellow Dodge in the parking lot. Cam waved to him and drove away. When he came back to work that night, he noticed the car again, parked in the same space. After a couple of days, it dawned on him that this car had not moved. The fellow in it always waved cordially to Cam as he came and went. What was the man doing sitting in his car for three days in the terrible cold and snow?

Cam discovered the answer the next morning. This time as Cam walked near the car, the man rolled down his window. He introduced himself and said he had been in his car for days with no money or food. He had driven to Fort Worth from out of town to take a job. But he arrived three days early and couldn't go to work right away.

Very reluctantly, he asked if he might borrow a dollar for a snack to get him by until the next day, when he would start work and get a salary advance. "I didn't have a dollar to lend him; I barely had gas to get home. I explained my situation and walked to my car, wishing I could have helped him."

Then Cam remembered his Grand Ole Opry dollar. He wrestled with his conscience a minute or two, pulled out his wallet and studied the bill one last time. Then he walked back to the man and gave him his bottom dollar.

"Somebody has written all over this," the man said, but didn't notice that the writing was dozens of autographs. He took the bill.

"That very morning when I was back home trying not to think about what I had done, things began to happen," Cam told me. "The phone rang; a recording studio wanted me to do a commercial that paid five hundred dollars. It sounded like a million. I hurried to Dallas and did the spot. In the next few days more opportunities came to me out of nowhere. Good things kept coming steadily, and soon I was back on my feet."

The rest, as they say, is history. Things improved dramatically for Cam. His wife had a baby and named him Joshua. Cam opened a successful auto-body shop and built a home in the country. And it all started that morning in the parking lot when he parted with his bottom dollar.

Cameron never saw the man in the old yellow Dodge again. Sometimes he wonders if the man was a beggar— or an angel.

It doesn't matter. What matters is that it was a test, and Cam passed.

Robert J. Duncan
Submitted by Jan Landis

The Man in Black

Although there have been many, this story is about meeting one of my special unsung heroes—*The Man in Black*.

It happened back in 1967. I dropped out of school and my parents told me I had two choices: one was to go back to school, the other was to join the Job Corps and learn a trade. Well, because the Job Corps would get me an airplane ride and I wouldn't have to mind my parents— besides, it was an adventure just like any immature kid would want—I opted for the Job Corps. Like most kids that age, I thought I knew it all, but I really didn't know anything! A couple of weeks later I was on my way to Rodman Job Corps Center in New Bedford, Massachusetts. For a boy from Kansas City, it was a completely new experience. There was ocean all around the Job Corps center, and as a kid from the Midwest, it was awesome. But it was nothing like home and it didn't take long before I was homesick.

My parents had brought me up listening to country— Hank Williams, Kitty Wells and yes, even Johnny Cash. So when I heard that Johnny was having a show around the New Bedford area, I saved up my money for two weeks—

just enough to see the show. Back then, it wasn't so much that I even liked his music, but that it was something that reminded me of home.

The night of the show, I took the bus that runs from the center to the downtown area to the theater where the show was going to be. I couldn't believe how many people were waiting to get into that theater. The seating was "first-come, first-served" so the line must have been two blocks long. Luckily it didn't take too long for me to get up near the front of the line. I got a pretty good seat to watch the show and the show went by real fast. Before I knew it, it was 11:00 P.M. But being that I was having fun it didn't matter.

Then I remembered the last bus going back to the center had already left. I was in trouble. There was no other way back except by cab and I had spent all my money on the ticket for the show. To make matters worse, if I didn't get back to the Job Corps center by 12:30 A.M., they would put me on restriction for a month. That meant that I couldn't go back to town for a month.

Because I was already in trouble and couldn't see a way out of it, I decided that I might as well go for broke and try and get Johnny's, June's, and everybody else's autograph that I could, because I would be stuck at the center for a month.

That is what I thought at the time. But that is not how it turned out.

When the show was over, everybody tried to get Johnny's and June's autographs. But I was a little craftier. I snuck past their security guards and got back into their dressing room. I ran into the dressing room thinking that no one would be in there and was startled when I ran into the Carter Family. The thing that got my attention was mother Mabelle. She had the most beautiful blue eyes I have ever seen. One of the girls asked me what I was doing there, and I told her I wanted to get Johnny's autograph. But before she could say anything, in walked Johnny and June.

The girl said, "This is ..."

"My name is Richard," I said.

"Where are you from, son?" Johnny asked in that deep southern baritone voice.

"Kansas City, sir," I replied. I was in awe. Here I was actually talking to *The Man in Black.*

"Why'd you come back here?" he asked.

"I wanted your autograph, sir," I managed to get across my lips.

He sort of smiled and said, "I think that can be arranged. ... Let me step in here and change, and I'll give you an autograph."

When he came back out, he said, "Okay, son, what would you like me to autograph?"

Well, I felt kind of stupid 'cause I hadn't brought anything for him to sign! I noticed a handball, picked it up, and he signed it for me.

He was getting ready to leave and he asked *me* if I wanted to carry his guitar out to his car! Needless to say, he didn't have to ask twice! I felt like I had the whole world in my pocket. I mean, here I was—*me*—carrying *Johnny Cash's guitar to his car!*

Well, off we were to his car. The only problem was he had forgotten where he had parked it. He remembered it was parked on the side of a restaurant, but he couldn't remember which side. He remembered that there was a sign with a blue whale picture on it. I knew where that was, so we were able to find his car.

He put his guitar in the trunk of his car and was getting ready to leave and all of a sudden he looked up at me and asked, "Where are your parents?"

"Back in Kansas City, sir," I told him.

"Well, how did you get to my show?" he asked inquisitively.
At that point, I told him the trouble I was in.

Without hesitation he asked, "Do you know how to find your way back to the center?"

I said, "Yes, sir. I know what streets to take there."

He said, "Well, get in, son, I'll drop you off there."

And with that, he took me back to the Job Corps center.

Now how many entertainers of his caliber do you know that would take the time out to help a kid like me stay out of trouble and make sure that they got home safe? There may be others, but from a personal point of view, I know only one—*The Man in Black*—Johnny Cash. My unsung hero.

So Johnny, if you're reading this, I just want to thank you for caring about that kid from Kansas City. Because you cared, it has given me a reason to care. Like I said, *it takes one to teach one.*

Richard Tripp

O Holy Night

A man never so beautifully shows his own strength as when he respects another's weakness.

Douglas Jerrold

The International Country Music Fan Fair in Nashville is always a zoo-like affair with three hundred or more people waiting in line at John Berry's booth for autographs, to take pictures, and to buy memberships and T-shirts. Fans often climb over the stanchions trying to get a picture and yelling at John to get his attention.

Last year, John and his wife, Robin, had a great idea for the theme of his booth. They felt it would be nice to have people come and visit them on their front porch, so they had the booth made as an identical replica of the porch on the Berry house. The display kind of depicts how John feels about his fans—almost like they're family. Coming onto his front porch at the show was a very comfortable thing for people.

Fan Fair began on Tuesday with a full day of interviews followed by over four hours of autograph signing at the booth. John's fan club party didn't close down 'til 2:30 the next morning.

John started Wednesday with the Capitol Nashville Showcase. After that, it was back to the booth where the autograph line began in front of the picket fence leading to the porch. A separate handicapped area fed into this line. At one point, I spoke with a woman who explained that she was deaf. She told me how she listened to John's music by laying her fingertips on the speakers in her home. Now, she just wanted to be face-to-face with John. She asked if she could touch him to really feel what she had been "hearing" through the speakers with her hands.

I was impressed by the woman who seemed like a kindly soul with a gentle spirit. In spite of her handicap, she was independent, positive and confident. Although I knew John was already exhausted, I was certain he'd want to meet this special fan. I took the woman over to John, let him know she was deaf and explained that she had a special request. John had her sit down next to his rocking chair and got very close. Everyone around kind of stepped back and things quickly got very quiet. The woman reached up and put her fingertips on John's throat. At that point, she asked him to sing. Without hesitation, and in the middle of June, John broke into "O Holy Night."

You could see a total transformation on the woman's face; and then the tears began streaming out of both of them. Everyone in the surrounding booths stopped talking, walking and taking pictures. All of us just watched. It was as if everything in the room had frozen except the two of them.

At the end of the song, there was a poignant pause followed by tumultuous applause and a standing ovation for the special moment that all had shared. John reached over and gave the woman a very tender hug. All of us felt the energy pass through them. The woman didn't say much after that. Within a moment, she found her friend and was gone.

Jean Calvert

The Chain of Love

Just to be alive and to be of service to somebody is a reward.

Jo Ann Cayee

He was driving home one evening, on a two-lane country road. Work in this small Midwestern community was almost as slow as his beat-up Pontiac. But he never quit looking. Ever since the Levi's factory closed, he'd been unemployed, and with winter raging on, the chill had finally hit home.

It was a lonely road. Not very many people had a reason to be on it, unless they were leaving. Most of his friends had already left. They had families to feed and dreams to fulfill. But he stayed on. After all, this was where he buried his mother and father. He was born here and knew the country. He could go down this road blind and tell you what was on either side, and with his headlights not working, that came in handy. It was starting to get dark, and light snow flurries were coming down. He'd better get a move on.

You know, he almost didn't see the old lady, stranded on the side of the road. But even in the dim light of day, he could see she needed help. So he pulled up in front of her Mercedes and got out. His Pontiac was still sputtering when he approached her. Even with the smile on his face, she was worried. No one had stopped to help for the last hour or so. Was he going to hurt her? He didn't look safe—he looked poor and hungry.

He could see that she was frightened, standing out there in the cold. He knew how she felt. It was that chill that only fear can put in you. He said, "I'm here to help you, ma'am. Why don't you wait in the car, where it's warm. . . . By the way, my name is Joe."

Well, all she had was a flat tire, but for an old lady, that was bad enough. Joe crawled under the car looking for a place to put the jack, skinning his knuckles a time or two. Soon he was able to change the tire. But he had to get dirty, and his hands hurt. As he was tightening up the lug nuts, she rolled down her window and began to talk to him. She told him that she was from St. Louis and was only passing through. She couldn't thank him enough for coming to her aid. Joe just smiled as he closed her trunk.

She asked him how much she owed him. Any amount would have been all right with her. She had already imagined all the awful things that could have happened, had he not stopped. Joe never thought twice about the money. This wasn't a job to him. This was helping someone in need, and God knows there were plenty who had given him a hand in the past. He had lived his whole life that way, and it never occurred to him to act any other way. He told her that if she really wanted to pay him back, the next time she saw someone who needed help, she could give that person the assistance that they needed, and Joe added, "and think of me."

He waited 'til she started her car and drove off. It had been a cold and depressing day, but he felt good as he headed for home, disappearing into the twilight.

A few miles down the road the lady saw a small café. She went in to grab a bite to eat and take the chill off before she made the last leg of her trip home. It was a dingy looking restaurant. Outside were two old gas pumps. The whole scene was unfamiliar to her.

The waitress came over and brought a clean towel for her to wipe her wet hair. She had a sweet smile, one that even being on her feet for the whole day couldn't erase. The lady noticed that the waitress was nearly eight months pregnant, but she never let the strain and aches change her attitude. The old lady wondered how someone who had so little could be so giving to a stranger. Then she remembered Joe.

After the lady finished her meal and the waitress went to get her change from a hundred-dollar bill, the lady slipped right out the door. She was gone by the time the waitress came back. She wondered where the lady could be, when she noticed something written on a napkin. There were tears in her eyes, when she read what the lady wrote. It said, "You don't owe me a thing. I've been there, too. Someone once helped me out, the way I'm helping you. If you really want to pay me back, here's what you do. Don't let the chain of love end with you."

That night when she got home from work and climbed into bed, she was thinking about the money and what the lady had written. How could she have known how much she and her husband needed it? With the baby due next month, it was going to be hard. She knew how worried her husband was, and as he lay sleeping next to her, she gave him a soft kiss and whispered soft and low, "Everything's gonna be alright. I love you, Joe."

Jonnie Barnett and Rory Lee

[EDITORS' NOTE: *This is a true story derived from the song of the same name.*]

A Special Gift

During the holidays, I sometimes think of Ol' Art. That wasn't his real name. It's just what we fifth-graders called the scrawny, likable classmate with the goofy smile, threadbare pants and poorly mended shirts.

Not that Ol' Art's poverty meant much in our rural Georgia area. Few people had money, but most had gardens, a pig for yearly meat and a willingness to share. The problem was Ol' Art's mom. She saw such offers as charity and stoutly refused any aid.

Still, Ol' Art never complained about carrying buttered biscuits for lunch, cheerfully washing them down with water from the hall fountain. The only time Ol' Art thought about his poor state was after suffering a bout of Lila's taunts. Lila, a local grocer's daughter, jeered at us all, but she seemed to take special pleasure in tormenting Ol' Art. She was in rare form when Ol' Art drew my name for the fifth-grade gift exchange during the upcoming school Christmas party.

"You won't even get a used head scarf this year!" Lila crowed, referring to a hand-me-down I received the previous year at the school's annual gathering. "Ol' Art here couldn't afford a box of dirt."

Ol' Art blushed beet red to the tips of his hair. He blinked fast and crossed his arms tightly against his thin chest, using his bony hand to try to cover the new hole in his shirt sleeve. Feeling awkward and ashamed ourselves, we all looked the other way. I wanted to comfort Ol' Art by reminding him it was Christmas, not presents, that mattered. However, I was a clumsy ten-year-old, too shy to say something so intimate to a boy.

Ol' Art's gift, wrapped in pieces of toilet tissue held together by a piece of twine, heightened Lila's mean giggles. However, she stopped midlaugh, her eyes growing wider than my own, when I pulled from that wad of tissue a sparkling rhinestone bracelet with a gold-plated heart attached. Hanging in the middle of the heart, a miniature gold cross was embedded with a red stone. It was, at that point, the most beautiful thing I had ever seen. I had never dared then to hope for such a possession, even in my dreams.

In fact, like the vagaries of a dream, something familiar tried to tug at my psyche as I stared at the bracelet, but the mental image would not come clear in my state of surprised pleasure. Slightly dazed, I glanced up to see that even the teacher was staring in open-mouthed wonderment at Ol' Art. He was smiling so hard in return it seemed as if his face might soon split with the effort. His happy grin lasted that entire afternoon. When Ol' Art's mom came to walk him home later, her usually grim expression softened at the sight of Ol' Art, and, going out side by side, a slight bounce in her step implied she shared her son's ecstasy.

His mom died the following year, and Ol' Art was taken in by relatives in another state. We never saw him again, but I never forgot him or that bracelet. It was eons later, after years of adulthood, that I ran across that bracelet again. The rhinestones had blackened with age, and the gold-plated heart was scratched and worn; but when I polished the bracelet, the red stone embedded in the miniature gold cross still gleamed.

"How," I finally asked after so many years, "did a fifth-grade boy who ate biscuits and water for lunch afford such a gift?"

It was then when an almost-forgotten sense of familiarity from the past became clear. About a month before that same Christmas party, I was in the school bathroom when I overheard a teacher outside the door ask the woman who had been hired to scrub floors for that day if she wouldn't like to take off her bracelet before beginning.

"I don't take it off until I absolutely have to," the woman had replied, almost apologetically. "My husband gave it to me before he died. I found out later he had sold his father's watch to get the money to buy it. I don't usually take off this bracelet for any length of time without good reason."

Making this mental connection at last, I realized Ol' Art's mom had eventually felt a compelling enough reason to not only remove her bracelet, but to give it up for good. That reason had been a mother's love. That love was so strong she wanted her son, the poorest boy in the class, to have one shining moment of glory when he was able to give the best gift at the school Christmas party.

Marijoyce Porcelli

The Trophy

The greatest happiness of life is the conviction that we are loved.

Victor Hugo

My dad had eight children, and Mama was pregnant again. Her labor had started. The hospital, in Lubbock, Texas, was about thirty-five miles away, and on the way to the hospital, my mother passed away. The baby inside her didn't make it either. I was four years old.

After that, my financially strapped dad put me and two of my brothers in the Methodist orphanage in Waco. That was to be our "home" for the next five years. As dad and my five older brothers and sisters drove away, a simple question took form in my young mind: *What will happen to me?* I can't begin to describe my panic and fear at not knowing the answer to that question. Placed in the care of total strangers, my brothers and I were devastated.

The three of us were housed in the infirmary for the first six weeks—separated from the rest of the children. Of course, nobody bothered to explain to me or my brothers what was going on or what we could expect next. The three of us were overwhelmed with feelings of loneliness and desolation, with no one to turn to for solace.

Later, my brother Jerry and I were placed in the same dormitory with about forty other kids. Delmar, my other brother who was about four years older than I, was sent to another dormitory. Each dormitory was under the supervision of an overworked matron with absolutely no time for nurturing her charges. At times, I'd sit alone in the dorm while billows of loneliness swept over me. It seemed as if *nobody* cared. It was like being in prison—or worse.

While we were in the orphanage, my brothers and I never really had anything we could call our own. If we got an apple or an orange at Christmas, we considered ourselves very lucky. But some say doing without is wonderful preparation for making someone glad for the "little things." I'll never forget Christmas at the orphanage when I was nine years old. A mystery friend gave me and my brothers a brand-new leather football. We were amazed to think that someone—anyone—had remembered us. That was one of the best Christmases of my entire life!

The following year, I moved back in with my dad. At the age of ten, I was old enough to "earn my keep." And I did—in spades! I'll never forget my thirteenth birthday, the day I picked 329 pounds of cotton on that West Texas farm. My dad gave me twenty-five cents. I'm still not sure whether the money was a birthday present or a reward for my labor!

Well, I took that twenty-five cents and went to see a movie, *Public Cowboy #1*, starring Gene Autry, "The Singing Cowboy." Afterward, I remember thinking to myself, *I could make a living doing that!* All I needed to get started was money for a guitar. (I've still got the poster from that movie hanging on my office wall.)

The first chance I got to make real money—money I could keep and spend for myself—was plucking turkeys for three to eight cents a bird in Clovis, New Mexico, during summer vacations. I lived in Whiteface, Texas—about sixty miles from Clovis. Pretty soon, I racked up enough turkeys to buy myself a $6.25 guitar and a 25¢ instruction book. From then on, every spare minute, I practiced with my guitar and worked on songs. When I was fifteen, I won a contest sponsored by KICA, the Clovis radio station. As the winner, I was given a live fifteen-minute program that aired every Saturday afternoon. Just me and my guitar. 'Course, there wasn't any money—the exposure and the experience were my pay. For the next three years, I hitch-hiked back and forth between Whiteface and Clovis every Saturday just so I could do this free program. For some reason, I never had any trouble getting from Whiteface to Clovis, but on the way back I sometimes couldn't get any closer to home than Morton—the nearest town on the main highway. From there, I'd have to walk the last ten miles. People tell me that's called "paying your dues." As I walked those long, lonely miles alongside the cotton fields of the Texas Panhandle, I can tell you, I felt like I was paying enough dues to last a lifetime!

After high school, I got gigs in a lot of clubs and even played rhythm guitar at several recording sessions for Columbia Records in Nashville. My first real break came when I was nineteen. Country star Hank Thompson hired me to be his opening act. That led to my first recording contract on Capitol Records.

In 1952, I started working on *The Louisiana Hayride*—a television show about equal in ratings with *The Grand Ole Opry*—where I stayed about three and a half years before moving on to *The Ozark Jubilee* for another three and a half years.

I had a memorable year in 1954 when "The Billy Walker Show" went on tour. One of our featured performers was a new face on the country music scene—Elvis Aron

Presley. On Elvis's birthday, January 8, 1955, I bought him a cupcake and put a candle in it.

In the years since then, I've been privileged to entertain millions of country music fans from the Hollywood Bowl to the Garden State Arts Center outside New York City and, as they say, around the world. In 1960, I was honored by induction as a member of The Grand Ole Opry.

Looking back—all things considered—I've had a wonderful life. In 1975, I came to understand that God has been looking after me all these years—even during those desperate times at the Methodist Home in Waco. Along the way, I've collected more than my fair share of trophies. But among all the certificates, banners, gold records, photographs and other prizes, there's only one treasure that holds the place of honor on the mantel over my fireplace—that special football.

Billy Walker

Ole Charley

I can still see him meandering down the long hill from the adult psychiatric ward to our cottage backyard where we took the children with autism out to play. His name was Charley, or "Charwee," as he pronounced it. I saw him every day for three years, and he always approached me with, "Hi, I'm Charwee. What's your name?" He would laugh, shake my hand and pat me on the head. "Hello, Joe!" was his childlike response, always with a hearty laugh and a warm smile . . . not to mention a wad of "bakker," or Skoal, in his mouth minus a tooth or two.

Charley rarely missed our afternoon recess. He loved playing with the autistic kids . . . running and laughing, eating dirt, leaves and various other nonedible items. Charley loved those kids and they loved him, too. So did I. He was a gentle ol' soul. He had been institutionalized for many years and he was mentally challenged; but that hearty laugh and smile were contagious.

However, one crisp autumn morn Charley 'bout cost me my job. My teacher's aide was out sick, and I had no backup that morning; so I was left to fend for myself with four young autistic children, two of whom were not even toilet-trained. That morning was destined to be the long-est four hours of my life.

By 8:30 A.M., the kids sensed the kill. Yes, they were in a state psychiatric hospital, but they were smart enough to know I could not handle all four of them by myself. Why not pay me back for all those times . . . I was about to explode when suddenly a loud knock came from our side door.

"Hi, I'm Charwee. What's your name?" After our usual exchange, Ole Charley, who rarely talked, whispered in my ear, "Got an itchin' you was in trouble and thought you could use my help." I stopped dead in my tracks, having never heard my friend utter much more than his name. Before I could question Charley, he was off, rubbing the kids' heads and laughing that laugh.

Within minutes, the classroom went from "Let's get him. . . ." to "Let's show Charwee what we're learning!" It was amazing! Charley had those kids eating out of the palm of his hand. So much so, that I decided to take a quick bathroom break, and . . .

I wasn't gone forty-five seconds. I raced back into the classroom to find my boss, the CEO for children and youth services, and an institute administrator, "taking a tour of the outstanding program we have for autistic children." My boss looked at me with eyes that cried out, "What in the world is going on here?"

"Yes, we met 'Charwee,'" our CEO sternly replied as she looked at me with eyes that could kill.

It seems Charley and the crew couldn't resist the combination of my absence and the old sink in our classroom, not to mention the four rolls of toilet paper and . . . It's amazing what four autistic children and one jolly old man can do with a faucet, toilet paper and forty-five seconds.

"Is Charley one of ours or one of yours?" the institute administrator questioned.

"He's a joint effort," I quickly chimed in as Charley and the boys sheepishly sat down at the table.

"A what effort?" my boss muttered, perhaps wondering if I had been dipping into Charley's Skoal can.

"I'm Joe's classroom aide," gleamed Charley. "We were conducting an experiment to see how the kids would respond in his absence."

"Absence?" My boss was now dumbfounded.

"Bathroom break," I sheepishly replied.

"Go poo poo!" yelled Donnie, the ringleader of the autistic crew.

"Good boy, Donnie!" hollered Charley as he grabbed Donnie's hand and led him out the classroom door to the bathroom.

"A joint effort, huh," the administrator sighed. "I wasn't aware of such a thing. Dr. Biggs," the administrator turned to our CEO, "looks like another one of your innovative ideas. You guys never cease to amaze me with what you can do with these kids."

"Yeah . . . amazing," my boss muttered under her breath.

Charley looked back at me with a gleam in his eye that was both haunting and heartwarming. He had almost buried me in one moment and saved my rear end in another.

"Conducting an experiment?" I questioned him. "I'm Joe's teacher's aide? Charley, you've never used big words like that before. What's going on?"

"Hi, what's your name?" he turned to me with that haunting gleam in his eye. "My name's Charwee."

At that moment it dawned on me I didn't know this jolly old man even though I had spent countless hours with him on our playground. Where did he come from, and why was he here in a mental institution?

That afternoon, I visited Charley's other world . . . his fourth-floor ward in one of the archaic adult psych buildings overlooking the sprawling acres and cottages below, where the children and youth programs were located. Behind an old, glassed-in nursing station reminiscent of *One Flew over the Cuckoo's Nest,* I read his chart. Charley was fifty-two years old. When Charley was twenty-six, his father had suddenly died and Charley, who was slightly retarded, was dropped off at the state hospital by his mom. She never came back to get him.

In the blink of an eye, Charley lost his family. In another blink of an eye, twenty-six years had gone by and Charley had not one visitor from the outside world . . . not one. Charley's best friend was an old blind woman named Irene, who amidst the howls of patients who truly needed to be on the unit, sang "Amazing Grace" with clarity and grit. I can still hear her raspy yet heavenly voice belting out those chords above the helter-skelter sounds of that eerie ward.

And what about Ole Charley? Well, he continued to sneak off from his world and meander down to our autistic neighborhood. "Hi, I'm Charwee. What's your name?" he would say and eagerly await my reply. "Hello, Joe!" he would laugh as he shook my hand and patted me on the head.

Ole Charley never used big words again around me. He kept things simple. And the kids . . . well, they didn't care about Charley's words. They simply loved his laughter and playfulness, his zest for dirt and toilet paper and old faucets and . . .

I would catch Charley watching me every now and then . . . that gleam in his eye, as if to say, "I saved your hide that day." I knew that he knew.

Ole Charwee.

My teacher's aide.

My loyal friend.

Joe Pritchard

They're Waving at Me

Every year, I experience an odd moment shortly after my family and I arrive at the country house we rent in Montana.

I drive down a back road, minding my own business, when I gradually realize that people are waving at me. They wave from their pickups and cars, barely lifting their hands off the steering wheel. At first the gesture is unsettling. I wonder if they are trying to tell me my lights are on or a tire is flat. Or perhaps it is a case of mistaken identity. I've never seen most of these people, so who do they think they are waving at?

Then I remember. I'm not in the city anymore. And if anything distinguishes city folk from country folk, it's that in rural areas people make a habit of waving at strangers.

Soon I'm waving at everyone too. I lift my fingers a little from the steering wheel, and the other driver lifts his. Or I shift my arm outward a bit as it rests on the window frame, raising my palm, and the other driver does likewise. One needn't be too obvious or exuberant about these things. A raised index finger speaks volumes, and a simple nod is eloquent in its restraint.

When I pass our neighbor, he salutes me with his customary broad, slow wave, which makes him look as
though he's cleaning a window. His wife waggles her
fingers to wave hello; I can almost imagine her saying
"Tootle-ooo!" A detective with the sheriff's office waves as
though he's firing a six-shooter—with the thumb up and
a quick jab of the index finger. (I'm still waiting for him to
blow away the smoke.)

People in the country will wave whether they're going
sixty miles an hour or ten. They wave on narrow curves,
on the crests of hills or driving into a blinding sun. Often
they wave in town when they should be watching for
pedestrians. In short, they wave at all the times it's most
inadvisable to wave.

If for some reason I forget to wave back—say I'm
fiddling with the radio dial—I can't help but feel a twinge
of guilt. Did the people who just waved know me? Were
they neighbors? Do they think I'm putting on airs? I
worry that I've violated one of the cardinal principles of
the universe, ordained when the first good person waved
hospitably to another from his cave.

To understand the geographical nature of this custom,
try a simple test: Wave from your car at strangers along a
city street. You may be stared at as if you are crazy. But
most likely you will be ignored. I also suspect that if a city
person spent a couple of weeks on country roads, he'd be
waving just as much as any dairyman, cowboy, logger,
beekeeper—or darn-fool visitor like me.

The reason is that, in the country, the human figure
stands out against the landscape; it demands recognition.
A wave is simply the easiest way of confirming that recognition. But I think waving is also a way of recognizing the
setting around the human figure.

I wave at the farmer passing me in a pickup, and my
wave extends to the grasses swaying along the roadside,

the line of trees tossing in the wind, the billowing white clouds. I wave, and my wave goes all the way to the horizon.

And so, as long as I'm in the country, I'm a dedicated waver. Howdy, I wave to the far range of mountains. Howdy, I wave to the horses trotting in the fields. Howdy, I wave to the kids and dogs romping in the yard.

When I pull into the driveway, my wife waves from the porch. Then she tries to teach our baby daughter to do the same. Howdy, I wave to them. Howdy, I wave. Howdy! Howdy!

Robert Crum

"Don't worry, it's just a barn dance."

The Farm Horse That Became a Champion

If you had been one of the thirteen thousand spectators at the National Horse Show in New York's Madison Square Garden in November 1959, you would have experienced an unexpectedly moving moment. In the middle of the evening, the arena was cleared, the lights were dimmed and the band struck up a triumphal march. All eyes followed a spotlight toward the entrance gate at the west end of the ring.

There a big gray horse—obviously not a Thoroughbred—appeared, preceded by five small children. As a blond young man and his wife led the horse to the center of the huge arena, the audience rose and began clapping. The applause was deafening. The young couple and their children beamed and bowed their thanks, the horse stomped his feet, and the thunderous clapping went on and on.

The horse was Snow Man, and he was being declared the Professional Horsemen's Association champion in open jumping—one of the highest honors the horse-show world has to bestow. That he and his owners, the handsome de Leyer family, were receiving such wild cheering was enough to make even the coldest cynic believe in fairy tales.

Less than four years before, Snow Man had been on his way to the slaughterhouse, a tired farm horse that nobody seemed to want or care about. Fortunately, somebody did care—and this is the story of that caring.

One wintry Monday in February 1956, twenty-eight-year-old Harry de Leyer set out from his small riding stable at St. James, Long Island, for the weekly horse auction in New Holland, Pennsylvania. Harry had been brought up on a farm in the Netherlands and had always loved horses. In 1950, he married his childhood sweetheart, Joanna Vermeltfoort, and they came to the United States. With only a smattering of English, and $160 in capital, Harry and Joanna first tried tobacco farming in North Carolina, then worked on a horse farm in Pennsylvania. Soon the two young Dutch immigrants had a few horses of their own, and within five years Harry was offered the job of riding master at the Knox School for Girls on Long Island. Now the father of three children, he was interested, of course, in doing anything he could to build security for his family.

When Harry headed for the Pennsylvania horse auction that February day, he was aiming to buy several horses for the school to use. He arrived late, however; most of the horses had been sold. Wandering outside, he saw several sorry-looking animals being loaded into a butcher's van. These were the "killers"—worn-out work horses that nobody wanted, except the meat dealer. The sight made Harry sad. He felt pity for any horse, however useless, that could not live out its last years in a green pasture.

Suddenly, Harry spotted a big gray gelding plodding up the ramp. The horse was chunky, but lighter than the others, and there was a spirited pitch to his ears, a brightness in his eyes. Unaccountably, on instinct alone, de Leyer called to the loader to bring the horse back down.

"You crazy?" said the meat dealer. "He's just an old farm horse."

Probably, Harry thought. The animal's ribs showed, his coat was matted with dirt and manure, there were sores on his legs. Still, there was something about him. . . .

"How much do you want for him?" de Leyer asked.

That's how it all started. Harry de Leyer redeemed an old plug for eighty dollars.

The whole de Leyer family was out to greet the horse the next day. Down the ramp of the van he came, stumbling over his big feet. He looked slowly about, blinking in the bright winter sun. Then, ankle-deep in snow, covered with shaggy white hair, he stood still as a statue. One of the children said, "He looks just like a snow man."

They all set about turning Snow Man into a horse again. First they clipped him lightly, and then they washed him— three times. In a while, the horseshoer came. Finally, cleaned and curried and shod, Snow Man was ready for his training sessions as a riding horse.

Harry laid a dozen thick wooden poles on the ground, spacing them a few feet apart. To walk across the network of poles, a horse had to lift its feet high and space its steps. When Snow Man tried it, poles flew every which way, and he stumbled and wove.

But Snow Man learned fast. By spring, he was carrying the novice riders at Knox, and some of the girls even began asking for him in preference to the better-looking horses.

When school closed that summer, Harry de Leyer made what might have been the biggest mistake of his life: he sold Snow Man to a neighborhood doctor for double his money, with the understanding that the doctor would not sell Snow Man, except back to him. After all, Harry told himself, he was in the horse business.

Now Snow Man began showing a side that hadn't previously come to light. He insisted on jumping the doctor's
fences, no matter how high they were raised, and coming
home—cross-country over fields and lawns, through
backyards and gardens. Irate citizens called the police.
The doctor was glad to let de Leyer have Snow Man back.

The feeling was mutual. For in some strange way, de
Leyer had come to believe that he and Snow Man shared
a common destiny. Solemnly he promised himself never
again to part with the horse.

Now, with indication that Snow Man liked to jump, de
Leyer began giving him special schooling as a jumper.
With kindness and hard work, he helped Snow Man over
tougher and tougher obstacles. Finally, in the spring of
1958, de Leyer decided to put the big gray to his first real
test—at the Sands Point Horse Show on Long Island,
where he would compete with some of the top open
jumpers in the land.

Incredibly, out on the Sands Point jump course, Snow
Man could do no wrong. Again and again, spectators held
their breath, expecting the ungainly looking animal to
come crashing down on the bars—but he never did. By
nightfall of the second day of the three-day show, he had
achieved the seemingly impossible: He was tied for the
lead in the open jumper division with the great old cam-
paigner, Andante.

Then, with success so close, on his final jump of the
day, Snow Man landed with his feet too close together,
and a back hoof slashed his right foreleg. By the following
day, it would be swollen and stiff. But de Leyer wasn't one
to give up easily. He cut a section out of a tire tube,
slipped it over Snow Man's injured leg like a sock, tied up
the bottom and filled the tube with ice. All night long, he
kept the improvised sock full of fresh ice, telling Snow
Man over and over how they would win the next day.

When morning came, the leg was neither stiff nor swollen. And on the final round of the day Snow Man beat the mighty Andante!

Harry de Leyer now saw that he had a potential champion—possibly even a national champion. However, giving Snow Man a chance to prove it meant hitting the horse-show circuit in earnest, vanning to a new show each weekend, putting up big entry fees, riding his heart out—a long, tiring summer and autumn that could end in little reward. Moreover, a spot on Harry's tongue had started hurting, and that worried him. It would be easier to forget about championships. Still, after talking it over, Harry and Joanna decided that Snow Man deserved a try.

So, to Connecticut they went. Snow Man won at the Fairfield Horse Show and at Lakeville. Then to Branchville, New Jersey, but Harry was in no condition to ride a winner. His tongue was bothering him badly, and he had scarcely eaten for a week. Consequently, Snow Man had a bad day. Blaming himself for the big jumper's first loss, Harry de Leyer drove home that Sunday night gritting his teeth against his pain.

On Monday, he went to a doctor. On Tuesday, he entered a Long Island hospital to have a tumor removed from his tongue. On Saturday, he got the laboratory report: The tumor was malignant. It was the end of the life he had known, the end of Snow Man's quest for glory.

Harry drove to the Smithtown Horse Show, a few miles from his home, making plans to sell his horses. But somehow he would keep Snow Man. The horse would be turned out to pasture.

Sitting at the show, de Leyer heard his name announced over the loud-speaker: He needed to go home immediately. Harry's first thought was his children! His second—a fire! He sped home, wondering how much more a man could take. But when he turned into the driveway, the children were playing in the yard and there stood the house. Joanna was close to hysteria, however. A message had come from the hospital that Harry's laboratory report had been mixed up with another: The tumor was not malignant!

"All of a sudden," Harry says, "my life was handed back to me."

From then on, the summer and early fall became one happy rush toward more and more championships at important shows. And finally it was November, time for the biggest show of all—the National at Madison Square Garden.

The National Horse Show lasts eight days. Horses that lack either consistency or stamina are weeded out long before the final night. After seven days Snow Man was tied in the Open Jumper Division with a chestnut mare, First Chance. For their jump-off on the eighth day, the course was long and intricate. It wove around the Garden oval in four overlapping loops; it included quick turns and changes of direction—combinations that call for perfect timing and coordination.

First Chance went first. Whether it was the tenseness of the moment, the wear and tear from so many days of jumping or the difficulties of the course, no one can be sure. At any rate, First Chance "knocked" several barriers.

Now it was up to Snow Man to run a cleaner course. Slowly he headed for the first jump. De Leyer nudged him with his knees, and the big gray exploded over it. Now up and over Snow Man went, and up and over again. Over the brush jump, over the chicken coop, the hog's-back, the bull's-eye, the striped panel. There were a few touches, but far fewer than First Chance had made. Finally Snow Man approached the last jump.

Now Harry de Leyer sat up in the saddle and threw the reins across the horse's neck. He was showing, for everyone to see, that it was not he who was responsible for this great performance, it was the horse. Snow Man rumbled up to that final jump, and he thrust and he sailed and it was done! An old and unpedigreed farm horse had won it all—the National Horse Show Open Jumper Championship, the Professional Horsemen's Association Trophy and the American Horse Shows Association High Score Award. He was declared "Horse of the Year" in open jumping,

Then, in 1960, Snow Man was "Horse of the Year" once more. And if you had been one of the vast crowd that filled Madison Square Garden that November evening to watch the de Leyer family and their big gray receive the ovation, you, too, would have stood . . . and clapped . . . and perhaps even cried—for the victory of a horse and a man who cared.

Philip B. Kunhardt Jr.

Great Love

*Any definition of a successful life must include
service to others.*

George Bush

In the winter of 1990, I was asked to appear on a television talk show in Toronto, Ontario, Canada. At the end
of our first day of taping I was on my way back to my
plush, high-rise, cable-TV, twenty-four-hour room service
hotel, when I saw something I'd never seen before.

Lying on the sidewalk against a building in four inches
of snow was a man sleeping with only a cardboard blanket to keep him from being completely exposed to the
freezing cold. What really broke my heart was when I
realized that he wore no shoes or socks.

I thought to stop and help him but was not quite sure
what to do. As the traffic light turned green, it seemed life
was demanding that I move along. So I did. Back in the
"anything I wanted was mine" environment of my hotel, I
promptly forgot about the man on the street.

Several days later, prior to the morning taping, I was
having coffee and Danish in the green room at the station.

All of the "important" people had left the room and it was just me and the janitor remaining.

I had seen him quietly go about his business every day while I was there, and he never said a word except "Good morning" or "Can I get anything for you, sir?" He always had a smile to give to everyone. When I asked him how he was feeling today, he told me that he'd been having to ride his bike to work in the snow and that he'd been feeling rather sorry for himself . . . that is, until he saw a man sleeping down on the corner of Yonge Street and Bloor with just a piece of cardboard for covering from the cold and no shoes. I almost choked on my Danish as I heard him go on to relate how he was so moved with compassion for the man that he went around the corner to a store and bought the man a pair of socks and shoes.

As I heard his story, I saw in my mind a poster that used to be in an old friend's bedroom when I was a teenager. It was a picture of a child handing someone a flower and the caption read: "The smallest deed always exceeds the grandest of intentions."

I stood there wishing it was me who had bought the shoes and socks for the man, when they called my name to come to the set.

As I got to the studio, they were just concluding an interview with a social worker who specialized in benevolence for eastern Ontario. The social worker relayed a story about Mother Teresa, who when asked once how she had accomplished such great things in her life responded, "None of us can do anything great on our own, but we can all do a small thing with great love."

When I went home that day, I looked for the man on the street. He was gone, but I knew it wouldn't be long before someone took his place.

Michael Peterson

Simpler Times

The heart generous and kind most resembles God.

Robert Burns

In 1949, school let out for Christmas and Pedro and Emmett rode the school bus home, talking and thinking about Santa Claus. Emmett said that he had tried to be good and wanted a BB gun. Pedro had gotten old enough and big enough and bright enough to know that if Santa Claus was going to bring him his favorite toys, he needed to pray real loud so Mama, Daddy and Grandmama could hear him. He also knew that it helped to turn down the pages in the Sears & Roebuck catalog in the outhouse. But deep down, Pedro wanted to believe in Santa Claus just like his younger friend, Emmett.

Christmas morning arrived and there it was, the shiny brand new bicycle just like Pedro wanted. Also there was some fruit and a brand new Little Red Ryder BB gun. Pedro couldn't wait to show Emmett and headed to Emmett's house. Upon arrival, Emmett looked over at Pedro, barely able to speak, and said, "Pedro, Santa Claus didn't come. Either I've been bad, or he ran out of toys." Pedro could see the hurt in Emmett's eyes and hear the disappointment in Emmett's voice. Pedro, without thinking, replied, "Emmett, Santa did come. He thought you were spending the night with me, and he left your BB gun at my house. I was a-bringin' it to you."

Emmett grinned like a baked opossum and was excited as a bug in a tater patch. Emmett hugged Pedro, and Pedro hugged back. At nine years old, at that moment, Pedro once again learned there really is a Santa Claus.

On the way home on his new bike without his BB gun, Pedro kept thinking, *Please Mama, don't be mad,* and she wasn't.

Charles D. Williams, M.D.

A Christmas Guest

Grandpa Jones, a man I consider brilliant, once found a book of poetry in Germany. The book had been in a fire and the lower portion of it was burned. Consequently, some of the poems didn't include endings, and though the book had been translated into English, it was archaic— a couple of hundred years old anyway. So when Grandpa returned to the U.S., he said, "I really like this poem, but I don't know how it ends." He gave the poem to me, and I wrote the last verse. Then I gave it back to him.

I got with Bill Walker to do the melody to go behind the recitation, and I told Grandpa we were going to record and that night he needed to be in the studio. I guess he thought we were going to have his regular band with four or five people. He walked in and an entire orchestra was waiting.

"I'm in the wrong place," he said.

"No, you're not," I replied.

Grandpa said, "Then it must be the wrong week, wrong day."

And I said, "No, it's not. This is your band."

"Is that going to be on the record?"

When I told him yes, he said, "I ain't never been out-numbered like this."

I ran down charts with the orchestra while Grandpa sat around. The song was done in one take. . . .

It happened one day near December's end,
Two neighbors called on an old-time friend,
And they found his shop, so meager and mean,
Made gay with a thousand boughs of green,
And Conrad was sitting with face a-shine—
When he suddenly stopped as he stitched a twine
And said, "Old friends, at dawn today
When the cock was crowing the night away,
The Lord appeared in a dream to me
And said, 'I am coming your guest to be,'
So I've been busy with feet a stir,
Strewing my shop with branches of fir.
The table is spread and the kettle is shined
And over the rafters the holly is twined—
And now I will wait for my Lord to appear
And listen closely so I will hear
His step as he nears my humble place,
And I open the door and look on his face."
So his friends went home and left Conrad alone,
For this was the happiest day he had known.
For long since his family had passed away
And Conrad had spent many a sad Christmas day.
But he knew with the Lord as his Christmas guest,
This Christmas would be the dearest and best.
So he listened with only joy in his heart,
And with every sound he would rise with a start
And look for the Lord to be at his door
Like the vision he had a few hours before.
So he ran to the window after hearing a sound,
But all he could see on the snow-covered ground

Was a shabby beggar whose shoes were torn
And he said, "Your feet must be frozen and sore—
I have some shoes in my shop for you,
And a coat that will keep you warmer, too."
So with grateful heart the man went away—
But Conrad noticed the time of day;
He wondered what made the dear Lord so late
And how much longer he'd have to wait—
When he heard a knock and ran to the door,
But it was only a stranger once more,
A bent old lady with a shawl of black,
With a bundle of kindling piled on her back.
She asked for only a place to rest,
But that was reserved for Conrad's great guest,
But her voice seemed to plead, "Don't send me away,
Let me rest for a while on Christmas Day."
So Conrad brewed her a steaming cup
And told her to sit at the table and sup.
But after she left, he was filled with dismay,
For he saw that the hours were slipping away,
And the Lord had not come as he said he would,
And Conrad felt sure he had misunderstood,
When out of the stillness he heard a cry,
"Please help me and tell me where am I."
So again he opened his friendly door
And stood disappointed as twice before.
It was only a child who had wandered away
And was lost from her family on Christmas Day.
Again Conrad's heart was heavy and sad,
But he knew he could make this little girl glad,
So he called her in and wiped her tears
And quieted all her childish fears,
Then he led her back to her home once more.
But as he entered his own darkened door,
He knew that the Lord was not coming today

For the hours of Christmas had passed away.
So he went to his room and knelt down to pray,
And he said, "Lord, why did you delay?
What kept you from coming to call on me,
For I wanted so much your face to see."
When soft in the silence, a voice he heard,
"Lift up your head for I kept my word.
Three times my shadow crossed your floor;
Three times I came to your lowly door;
For I was the beggar with bruised cold feet;
I was the woman you gave something to eat;
And I was the child on the homeless street;
Three times I knocked, three times I came in,
And each time I found the warmth of a friend.
Of all the gifts, love is the best;
I was honored to be your Christmas Guest."

Grandpa Jones
Introduction by Fred Foster

Christmas Guest reprinted by permission of Loray El Marlee Publishing.

Momma's Christmas Magic

About twenty-five years ago, Christmas was much the same as it is now. A tree with lights. Midnight Mass. Christmas dinner. But times were hard for some families. I know they were hard for us because my brothers and I were orphans. My paternal grandmother had stepped in, and with very meager, sometimes nonexistent resources, she set out on a daunting journey to rear us. Having already gotten her own nine children off to a start and out of the nest, she felt up to the task. However, rearing three small children in the fifties and sixties was different than it had been in the thirties and forties, especially since her dear husband had passed, and she was alone.

Momma, as we all called her, was quite a character. Those of us who knew her remember her as having a quick wit and a hard-working, kind soul. She could make a grand meal out of nothing, and boy, did she love a game of cards! Even if she wasn't feeling well, she'd play "auction" all night long! Her bark was worse than her bite, although those of us who had been on the receiving end of it didn't think so at the time.

This one Christmas, however, things had gone from bad to worse. With no such thing as assistance available to her in those days, her only sources of income were a small Veterans allowance, our family allowance and her pension. With such limited funds, extras for three small children were in short supply. Thankfully, one of our relatives was a farmer, so some meat and fresh vegetables were usually available. But the light bill was overdue, the wood was running low and, to make matters worse, the oil tank was threatening to run dry.

Poor Momma was in quite a fix with all these problems to shoulder alone, and many nights when we went upstairs to bed, we heard her downstairs at the kitchen table lighting a cigarette, her only luxury, and drinking a cup of tea. She stared out the window at the dark, wishing I suppose for some sort of a miracle.

Well, I guess God listens to such wishes, for some sort of a miracle did happen. To a twelve-year-old child, it's kind of tough, I guess, knowing there isn't much for Christmas. I was glad my brothers were younger, one only a baby. They wouldn't realize the difference as long as Santa left something.

None of us kids could comprehend how serious things were until three or four days before Christmas when our water pipes froze from the cold, and all of a sudden, we were without water. Momma had been forcing herself to ration the wood and oil in an effort to make them last a bit longer, but the winter wind was relentless.

This seemed to be the last straw for her, with the added threat of the power being shut off, and still nothing for Christmas. She did something we had never seen her do before. She slowly walked over to her favorite chair at the end of the table, sat down heavily, folded her arms on the table, put her head down, and cried. Shuddering sobs so deep, and for so long, that we stopped our play and sat quietly. It scared us to see her so upset and utterly hopeless, and I think even as young as we were, it dawned on us that something was wrong.

As if on cue, we heard a knock at the door. Momma tried to compose herself. She smoothed down her ever-present apron and answered the door. She wasn't expecting anyone, certainly not the tall, thin, silver-haired gentleman who asked if he could come in. He sat and talked to her awhile; she seemed to know who he was, and we children went back to our play.

After a bit, he got ready to leave, and I guess to our young eyes he appeared taller than he actually was. Before he left, he reached into a deep pocket and took out a white envelope, which he pressed into Momma's hand. She thanked him gratefully, but left the envelope unopened until after the gentleman had gone. He wished us all a merry Christmas and then he left.

Hands shaking, she opened the envelope and looked inside. As if in a dream, she slowly sat down in her chair again, and once more put her face in her hands and cried.

This time, we all began to cry. It was too much. Frozen pipes, maybe losing our lights, fuel running low, Momma crying twice in one night, this time after a stranger passed her an envelope. What was in that envelope anyway. Another bill? More bad news?

With tears on her cheeks, Momma said, "No! No! Don't cry! It's wonderful news! See what's in this envelope? It's Christmas!"

She opened it up. Wow! A fresh, crisp one-hundred dollar bill. A fortune! Certainly in those days it was.

Well, poor Momma! She almost flew to the telephone and arranged a drive to town the next day. She was so happy, and we were so glad to see her smiling face again. She helped us get ready for bed, and indeed, the teapot went on the stove very quickly that night. Out came a pen and paper and as we went upstairs, a list was being compiled and a budget carefully stretched.

The next day, with the youngest of us in tow, the other two in school, Momma set off for town with her pre-arranged ride. Somehow, maybe more Christmas magic, that one hundred dollars bought a lot of happiness. First things first—the electric bill was secured and wood was ordered, some oil was dispatched to be delivered to the house, and she called a neighbor in to fix the pipes. With the necessities covered, she carefully rationed what was left.

On Christmas morning, excitement was pretty high. Santa had come! Something nice for everyone, and I can still remember what I received. It was a beautiful brown sweater with a butterfly design on the front. It was so warm, and I loved it. Also, a book for me I loved to read! The boys were so pleased with what Santa had left: trucks to play with, puzzles to put together, and no doubt a hockey stick had appeared, too.

In an effort to keep us all believing, there was even a pack of cigarettes under the tree for Momma. Given the circumstances, I'm sure it was her only comfort in those hard times.

Christmas dinner soon followed, and I honestly don't remember if we had a turkey. As I said earlier, Momma was a wizard at making the most out of nothing, but even one hundred dollars only goes so far. It didn't seem important, because whatever we had for dinner, we were warm and comfortable and so happy. I do remember the wonderful smell and delicious taste of Momma's brown sugar cookies and creamy fudge. She must have been up all night.

She was so relieved and happy after that. I'm sure she must have believed in Santa from then on, for in her darkest hour, her prayer had been heard and a miracle arranged.

Even after all these years, as a mother of four wonderful children of my own, I still remember that Christmas, and I can only imagine the despair she must have felt. I later learned the silver-haired gentleman was a local businessman and politician. His visit must have appeared to be a miracle to Momma, for how he knew of her troubles she could only guess. All he asked of her was that she was not to mention the deed to anyone, and she never did reveal his identity.

Since that long-ago Christmas, our benefactor well, he has passed away, and so has Momma, but there isn't a Christmas that goes by that we don't think about her. We still love her and miss her, and I think even through the struggles, she managed to instill in us a love for the Christmas season and a belief that God hears our prayers, and sometimes even answers them.

Nova MacIsaac

The Right Spirit

Our happiness is greatest when we contribute to the happiness of others.

Anonymous

As the mother of four children, I had my hands full. Christmas was a busy, hectic time. My four children were sprawled across the living-room floor, watching television and writing down their lists of Christmas presents they wanted. My three-year-old, Ally, had the Sears catalog open and was picking out toys for Santa to bring. Joshua, the ten-year-old, was describing in great detail the different "cool" toys from the popular *Men in Black* movie. Twelve-year-old Matthew had his worn baseball mitt in his hand and was showing his father and me how he needed a new one. And Chad, our nineteen-year-old son, was writing a long list that included everything from a leather jacket to a new set of golf clubs.

On the six o'clock news on television that evening was a special feature about families who needed help at Christmas. These were families who didn't have enough money for food, let alone Christmas presents. I noticed that all four of our children were glued to the story.

Joshua said, "Why don't we pick a family and help them out by each of us giving up one of our presents?"

"What do you mean?" I asked him, looking over sideways at my husband, to make sure he heard this, too.

"We always get so many gifts," Joshua said. "Maybe we could share some of our gifts with others."

"I think that's a wonderful idea," I said, somewhat surprised. Then, I turned to the other children and said, "What do the rest of you guys think?"

"Well, we are fortunate," Chad said. "It's hard to imagine that there are families out there who don't even have food. I think it's the least we could do, and I'm kind of ashamed we haven't thought about it before."

After a brief discussion, everyone agreed that giving to a needy family was the "right spirit" of Christmas. We telephoned the television station and told them we wanted to help out a family, preferably one with several children. We found the perfect family—one with four children ranging from a two-year-old girl to boys, nine, ten and eleven years old. The plan was for each of our children to shop and pick out a present for one of those children and give up that gift on their "wish" list.

The next night my husband and I took the children to a huge toy store. I had never seen them so excited about shopping! Ally headed directly for the play dishes, dolls and paint sets. She lovingly and carefully went through the items, searching for "just the right gift," and finally settled on a baby doll wrapped in a blanket that you could feed and cuddle.

She said, "Mommy, I know that little girl will love this baby because it's just like the one I wanted Santa to bring me."

My heart went out to her as I watched this kind, unselfish gesture.

Joshua found the display for the *Men in Black* toys and picked out a fierce machine gun that could blast aliens. It was one that he desperately wanted to have, but he agreed to give it to the little boy of the needy family, instead.

"I'll get plenty of gifts," he said, "and that little boy will love this!"

Our nineteen-year-old picked out some toy trucks and cars that he had loved when he was a boy—a red fire engine and an ambulance. He tested them in the store to make sure they made real siren sounds. What good was an ambulance or fire engine if it didn't have sirens? And Matthew found the perfect baseball mitt.

"All children need a baseball mitt!" he exclaimed. He couldn't imagine growing up and not playing baseball.

They all proudly marched up to the cash register with their gifts in their hands. I had never seen such joy in their faces as they put everything on the counter.

My husband and I watched our children that night with pride and love. When did they get to be so wise and giving of themselves? We weren't sure how, but we were raising four children who had discovered the "right spirit" at Christmas.

Merilyn Gilliam

The Chain

Some people come to Nashville and slowly lose sight of who they are. They forget the simple pleasures. They forget their roots. They forget their own story. They don't understand that we are all like links in a chain, connected to our past and connected to our future—our children.

My story starts like a lot of people's stories—with my dad. He is my link to the past, to a simpler time. My father was, and still is, a major influence in my life. He was a preacher and a man of great wisdom, strength and generosity. Although our family wasn't rich, it felt like we were rich because of the amount of love my father gave us and the way he expressed it. Now, learning to share with my own kids that wisdom my father passed along to me is my way of continuing that chain unbroken.

When I was a kid, a lot of folks were down on their luck. Often when they'd come into town, the first person these folks would call on was the preacher. I remember once when some people came to our house who didn't look particularly respectable. I called my dad and he came to the door. I heard our visitors tell their hard-luck story, and in my gut I knew they were being less than honest. In disbelief, I watched my dad give them money. After the whole thing was over and they'd left, I asked, "Do you really think those people were telling the truth?"

My dad said, "Honestly, Son, if I had to say 'yes' or 'no,' I'd have to say 'no.' But it doesn't matter."

"But telling the truth always matters," I said with that little-kid insistence that comes from always knowing more than your elders.

He said, "No, it doesn't matter, Son. What they were doing is what they were doing; and what we were doing is what we were supposed to do. They expressed a need, we had more than we needed, and so we gave to them. God will deal with us and what we do the same way he will deal with them and what they do. Really, the two things do not depend on each other."

My father's wisdom struck me. I think I've carried that wisdom with me into my life, and I think that is the way I want to live. Some people spend their whole lives "keeping score"—they feel they have to come out on top in every encounter. I'm sure there are lines that you can cross where you can be completely taken advantage of by strangers and even people you think are your friends. But you have to ask yourself, "Does it really matter?"

I'm the guy who always stops for the down-and-out men by the side of the road. Like many people, I assume that many of them are going to use my money to buy cigarettes or liquor—but I am still my brother's keeper. I have more than I need. I can give. And for every needy guy who doesn't use the money wisely, there's a deserving guy with an honest, hard-luck story that will break your heart.

I make sure my children know that it's important to stop and help. It's important to give at least a little bit everywhere you can. That's the part of Dad I pass along— my part of the chain.

In caring for our part of the chain, my family does work with the Make-A-Wish Foundation, a nonprofit

organization that tries to grant the simple wishes of ter-
minally ill children. For some youngsters, attending my
show is what they wish for. I've never turned anyone
down. My wife is also very involved with Make-A-Wish.
Sometimes, Make-A-Wish children come and stay at our
farm when it's close to their last weeks of life.

My own kids are five, eight, and ten and are at various
levels in understanding our efforts to ease the suffering of
others. My wife and I never cease to marvel at the way
our own children respond to seeing our acts of simple
kindness. Our children know that these Make-A-Wish
kids are dying, and they know what we're doing is—on a
grand scale—futile. They know what we're doing isn't
going to change the outcome dramatically, but they've
come to realize it's still the right thing to do. It's still giving what you can give. It's making your own little corner
of the world a little bit softer and nicer for someone else.

Sometimes, you're lucky enough to be able to show
kindness to people you know personally. For many
years, we employed a man who drove our tour bus. He
had a daughter with very serious health problems. After
receiving a lung transplant, she suffered a relapse and
eventually died at the age of fifteen. A few weeks before
this girl passed away, her dad brought her out to our
farm where I keep a small plane. Although the girl had
experienced emergency flights for surgery, she had not
been conscious during any of them. Her last wish was to
fly in a small plane.

The kids and I sat and talked to the girl and her parents
for a while before I took her up to fly. She had an oxygen
bottle with her containing a supply that was supposed to
be good for forty-five minutes or so. We climbed into my
little plane—a Piper Super Cub—where I got her and her
oxygen strapped into the backseat. If you've never flown
in a small plane, you'll have to trust me when I say it's one

of the great pleasures of life. You really are, to a large degree, free as a bird. It's as near to the Wright brothers' experience as you're going to get.

At the time we took off, it was that magical hour just before sunset. I could hear my young passenger start giggling. And she didn't stop giggling for the full twenty minutes we were in the air. She had this constant, sincere, but low-grade chuckle for the entire time. I think it was the freedom of it all—those moments of pain and struggle were all but forgotten in the air and we could just soar.

When we came back, the girl's oxygen bottle was almost completely empty. She had been back there breathing up her oxygen with the sheer happiness and thrill of the ride. There was more joy on her face at that moment than I can ever remember seeing on anybody's face. After she went home with her parents, my son asked, "Is she gonna die, Dad?"

I nodded my head solemnly.

"When I grow up, I want to be able to do things like this for other people. To make them happy," my son said.

It was then that I realized the chain was continuing— unbroken. Because that's exactly the way my dad taught me.

Gary Chapman

Teddy Bear

I was on the outskirts of a little southern town trying to reach my destination before the sun went down. The old CB was blaring away on channel 1-9 when there came a little boy's voice on the radio line. And he said, "Breaker one-nine, is anyone there? Come on back truckers and talk to Teddy Bear."

I keyed the mike and said, "You got it, Teddy Bear."

The little boy's voice came back on the air, " 'Preciate the break. Who we got on the other end?" I told him my handle and then he began. "Now I'm not supposed to bother you fellas out there. Mom says you're busy and for me to stay off the air. But you see, I get lonely and it helps to talk 'cause that's about all I can do. I'm crippled and cannot walk."

I came back and told him to fire up that mike and I'd talk to him as long as he'd like.

"This was my dad's radio," the little boy said. "But I guess it's mine and Mom's now 'cause my daddy's dead. Dad had a wreck about a month ago. He was trying to get home in a blinding snow. Mom has to work now to make ends meet. I'm not much help with my crippled feet. She says not to worry, that we'll make it all right. But I hear her crying sometimes late at night. Ya know, there's one thing I want more than anything else to see. Ah, I know you guy's are too busy to bother with me. But, ya see, my dad used to take me for rides when he was home. But I guess that's all over now since my daddy's gone."

Not one breaker came in on the CB as that little crippled boy talked to me. I tried hard to swallow the lump. It just would not stay down as I thought about my boy in Greenville Town.

"Dad was going to take Mom and me with him later on this year. Why, I remember him saying, 'Someday this ol' truck will be yours, Teddy Bear.' But I know I will never get to ride in an eighteen-wheeler again. But this old base will keep me in touch with all my trucker friends. Teddy Bear's going to back out now and leave you alone 'cause it's almost time for Mom to come home. But you give me a shout when you're passing through and I'll be happy to come back to you."

Well, I came back and said, "Before you go ten-ten, what's your home twenty little CB friend?" Well, he gave me his address and I didn't hesitate one second 'cause this hot load of freight was just gonna have to wait. I turned that truck around on a dime and headed for Jackson Street 229. As I rounded the corner, I got one heck of a shock. Eighteen-wheelers lined up for three city blocks. Why, I guess every trucker from miles around had caught Teddy Bear's call and that little boy was having a ball. For as fast as one driver could carry him in, another would carry him to his truck and take off again. Well, you better believe I took my turn at riding Teddy Bear. And then I carried him back in and put him down in his chair. Buddy, if I never live to see happiness again, I want you to know I saw it that day in the face of that little man. We took up a collection before his momma came home. Each driver said good-bye and then they were all gone. He shook my hand with a mile-long grin and he said, "So long trucker, I'll catch ya again."

I hit that interstate with tears in my eyes. I turned on the radio and got another surprise. "Breaker one-nine," came a voice on the air. "Just one word of thanks from Momma Teddy Bear. We wish each and every one a special prayer for you, 'cause you just made my little boy's dream come true. I'll sign off now before I start to cry. May God ride with you. Ten-four and good-bye."

Red Sovine

"TEDDY BEAR"
Written by Dale Royal, Tommy Hill, Red Sovine and J. William Denny
Copyright ©1976 Cedarwood Publishing
Used By Permission. All Rights Reserved.

Teddy Bear's Last Ride

I was there that day and I saw her cry . . . after Mama Teddy Bear said: "Ten-four and good-bye!" She turned off the old CB and just looked at me and her heart overflowed. Her tears ran free and the gratitude shone in her face like the sun for all the things these big tough truckers had done. A handful of change and a few dollar bills, but most of all, a little crippled boy's dream fulfilled.

I guess I was Mama Teddy Bear's best friend. I'd lived by her and little Teddy Bear since . . . oh, I couldn't remember when. And that's why now, before my memory grows old, the rest of the story just has to be told.

I'd come over and sit with Teddy Bear while his mama was away and play little games to help him pass the day. But in the afternoons he'd wheel that chair over by the radio and he'd go on the air. And I never knew a trucker not to answer his call. He'd just grin and ask me not to tell his mama, but I was pretty sure she knew what was going on.

Time has a way of taking its toll, and much too fast Mama Teddy Bear was growin' old—I watched as the silver touched her hair. But her one aim in life was Teddy Bear. And then I saw another change take place—Little Teddy Bear was slowly losing the race—and I knew it. His mama knew it, too. There was nothing in this whole world either of us could do.

He talked less often on the old CB. There were times when he would hardly talk with me. He took to sittin' by the window and watchin' the road, the big eighteen-wheelers rollin' by with their loads.

Finally he was too weak to get out of bed. One day he looked up at me and said: "Would you turn the radio on and go on the air and tell all my trucker friends what's happened to Teddy Bear?" Well, the hardest thing I've done in my time was to pick up that mike and say: "Breaker one-nine! This is for all you truckers who care. . . . I'm callin' for your little friend, Teddy Bear. He says to tell you he misses you all and he's awful sorry he can't answer your calls!"

They all came back and joked with me and said that they'd catch him later on the old CB. They never did catch Teddy Bear again, 'cause late one night the angel came and the last thing he said before he died was: "Tell all my trucker friends how I enjoyed the rides!" Mama Teddy Bear couldn't tell 'em and neither could I 'cause every time we'd look at that radio, we'd both start to cry.

The funeral was preached at the chapel and Little Teddy Bear started on his last ride. As the procession rounded the little city square, the sounds of a hundred engines filled the air. The truckers had dropped their trailers back somewhere behind, and one by one, they fell in line. They all tried to comfort Mama Teddy Bear, and it seemed like the warmth of God just filled the air.

Slowly they formed a circle around the little grave. A
lot of big men cried that day as they paid their respects
on Teddy Bear's last ride.

Dale Royal and J. William Denny

I Meant to Do That

*It is only when we truly know and understand
that we have a limited time on earth and that
we have no way of knowing when our time is up
that we will begin to live each day to the fullest,
as if it were the only one we had.*

Elisabeth Kübler-Ross

Before I got into the music business, I worked for a
couple of years as a registered nurse at the children's hospital back home in Canada. One of the patients I cared for
was a little girl named Aimeelee who was afflicted with a
severe case of cystic fibrosis. Because of her illness, she
was in and out of the hospital quite often.

As I got to know her, I discovered that Aimeelee was a
really amazing little girl. She was the kind of kid who, faced
with a critical illness at an early age, took advantage of
every single moment in her life. It was almost like she had
to grow up a lot in those last few years that she was alive.

While I worked at the hospital, I occasionally took time
off to visit Nashville as I made plans for a new career in
country music. Aimeelee thought my trips to Nashville

were really cool. Whenever I was back in Canada, Aimee-lee and I shared a lot together—she liked to write poetry and I wrote songs.

On one of my trips to Nashville, I wrote the song "I Meant to Do That." (The song deals with those things all of us intend to do but never quite find time for—such as saying "I love you" to those we care about.) When I returned to Canada from that trip, I learned that Aimeelee had gone back into the hospital and wasn't doing very well. When I walked into her room, I was struck by how frail she looked against a background of blinking, beeping life-support machines. Tubes fed oxygen to her nostrils and nourishment to her veins. Aimeelee's parents sat next to her bed and held her small hands. All the while, a steady stream of doctors and nurses moved in and out of the room providing constant care for the young patient.

I knelt beside Aimeelee's bed and took her hands in mine, realizing at that moment that I just needed to talk to her. As she faded in and out of consciousness, I asked, "Hey, Aimeelee, how are you doing?" The first thing she said was, "Hi, Paul! How was your trip to Nashville?" I couldn't believe it! This little girl was fighting for every single breath; and instead of complaining or feeling sorry for herself, she was more concerned with me than with anything going on in her room.

Later that night, one of my friends from work called and told me that Aimeelee had passed away. Aimeelee's attitude really blew me away and changed the way I looked at my own life. It made me think of how I was treating people and if I was taking advantage of every single moment—telling those close to me that I loved them whenever I had the chance.

Quite some time after Aimeelee's death, the video of "I Meant to Do That" was released. Not long afterward, I was a guest on a whole series of radio talk shows. While on these shows, I never failed to talk about my experience with Aimeelee and what I learned by her example. But what I found really rewarding was when my mother—who runs my fan club—got a call from Aimeelee's parents. They said they had heard me talking about Aimeelee during a radio show. They later wrote me a letter saying, "Thank you for letting Aimeelee's memory live on. It was because of your story on the radio that we felt her life really meant so much." They were able to see what an inspiration their daughter had been to other people.

Something else Aimeelee taught me—indirectly—was that while I want to be a successful businessperson and musician, more importantly, I want to be a successful human being. I want to be someone who has a successful spiritual life and family life. After all, those are the things that are going to last and are going to matter. Somebody might not remember a song I've written twenty or thirty years from now, but they're going to remember if I treated them the right way.

It's such a great feeling when I'm able to look out into the audience and see people wiping a tear away when I'm playing that song or telling Aimeelee's story. After the show, people often come up and tell me how that song helped them get through some difficult time. That's when I know that Aimeelee's life made a huge difference—and still does—in many people's lives. For me, being a part of that whole thing is very rewarding.

My wife, Liz, and I still have a picture of Aimeelee by our bed. When I wake up each morning, the picture reminds me to take advantage of every moment in life—just as Aimeelee did. That way, I'll never again have to say, "I meant to do that."

Paul Brandt

Raymond

When we look for the good in others, we discover the best in ourselves.

Martin Walsh

Raymond was that special kid, back in my hometown
He never did very well in school we'd laugh and poke fun
   at him
Give him lots of guff, you know how sometimes kids can
   be cruel
We had a nickname for Raymond, it made him so mad
   he'd turn red
And sometimes even cry, but we all thought it was pretty
Funny at the time when we'd choose up to play ball
Eigno-Raymond, was always the last name called
Eigno-Raymond, eigno-Raymond, we'd all laugh and say
Oftentimes he'd just drop his head, then slowly walk
   away
He'd wander over to the far side of the playground
And play by himself. We never gave much thought
To how Raymond must have felt

Well a lot of years have passed, and we've all gone
Our separate ways, but I can't help but feel ashamed
Now looking back on those days, I wish I'd been
Smart enough to be Raymond's friend and kinda
Help him through those hard times, he was living in
Especially now that I have a son. Hey, he's quite
A little man, one thing's for sure I'm gonna
Do everything I can do, to help him understand
That just because someone's a little different
Maybe in their color or their size, doesn't mean
They don't have feelings down deep inside
And just so I'd never forget that through
The good Lord's eyes we all look the same
On the day that my son was born, I chose
Raymond for his name.

Luke Reed and Phil Thomas

2

ON FAMILY

*A good country song taps into strong
  undercurrents of family, faith and
  patriotism.*

George Bush

Daddy's Little Girl

Sometimes I would rather have people take
away years of my life than take away a moment.

Pearl Bailey

When I heard the song "Daddy's Little Girl," every line
in the lyrics related to me. Daddy was a very big influence
in my life. Besides teaching me a good work ethic, he also
influenced me musically—he taught me how to play the
guitar. In spite of our closeness throughout my childhood
and in our relationship today, Daddy never really showed
a lot of physical affection towards me. As a former Marine,
showing emotion and hugging was never something that
came easy to him. He always demonstrated his love by
working hard, giving me encouragement to be a good person and providing for me.

All that changed the night of June 12, 1997. I was
scheduled to do a Father's Day show on TNN's *Primetime
Country*, and the producers wanted my father to be with
me as part of the program. They had asked me to sing
my song, "Daddy's Little Girl," and then do the normal
interview portion with Gary Chapman and my dad. The

interview segment was going to be a piece of cake, I thought, because I love to talk! However, the performance portion was creating real anxiety for me—not only because it would be my first time singing the song in front of my father, but sixteen years had passed since the last time he and I had hugged or said, "I love you."

So the big moment finally arrived. With just thirty seconds until I had to perform, I stepped from behind the curtain and onto the stage. There, in the front row of the auditorium, sat my dad.

As the piano introduction started, I could tell Daddy was fighting back the tears. I felt the professional thing to do was be tough and try to rise above the emotion I was feeling, but there was no way! The more I sang, the more sensitive I became. Overwhelmed, I heard my voice start cracking while uncontrollable sobs accompanied each line. As I got ready to sing the last verse, I saw that Daddy had tears streaming down his face. I just lost it! I walked into the audience to share Daddy's embrace as I sang through the ending of the song.

All those years without an "I love you" or a hug were all redeemed for us that night right there on national TV as millions of viewers shared that priceless moment.

Kippi Brannon

Mama Sang a Song

I was inspired to write "Mama Sang a Song" while sitting around my house not long after I'd moved to Nashville, thinking about my upbringing and my roots.

One thing many of us Southerners have in common is a memory of old-time camp revival meetings. The meeting that came to mind was one I attended in my teens, and it has stayed with me for years because of an unusual occurrence.

The Reverend Homer Rodeheaver, a well-known evangelist, had been at our church all week conducting services. A big part of what he did every night was to break out his big, loud trombone and lead the congregation in singing the old-time Gospel hymns.

The sanctuary of our church was shaped like a capital letter T, with the pulpit in the middle of the top bar, and the congregation off three sides. On this particular night, I was sitting with some of my teenaged friends in one of the smaller side sections, so we couldn't see much of the main congregation, nor the small balcony over the back.

But the Reverend could. He loved to try to get the congregation in each section to try to "outsing" the others. And he was in rare form that particular night.

The hymn Reverend Rodeheaver picked out for us to work on was the old favorite, "Brighten the Corner Where You Are."

"Let's just see which corner of this church we can brighten the most!" he boomed. "Let's see which group can sing the loudest!" And with that, he began blowing his trombone, the organist joined in, and the rafters really started ringing.

"Okay, let's start with the left side!" he said, and everybody over there opened up with "Brighten the corner where you are," at the top of their voices.

"Now the right side!"

And my buddies and I let it fly.

"Now the main floor!"

It practically sounded like an earthquake.

"Now the balcony!"

And suddenly there was silence. Silence, I should say, with the exception of one loud female voice, belting about four keys flat, "Bry-tun thu caw-nau whays you ahhhhh!" in the heaviest of Southern drawls.

I was told that the whole main body of the congregation suffered whiplash turning to the balcony to see where that awful voice was coming from. My buddies around me fell to the floor laughing. I'm sure I would have joined them, except for one stark realization—that voice was my mother's.

She and my sister had come in late and were the only ones seated upstairs.

Being a teenage boy, my reaction at the time was simple and predictable. I turned scarlet. I wanted to crawl under the pew and never come out.

But thinking back on it that day in Nashville as an adult, that mortifying incident came to mean something completely different than it ever had before.

I realized that my mother had simply done what she'd

always done. She had brought her faith and her love to the church the only way she knew how. There were dozens of people there that night who sang that song right on pitch, but perhaps they didn't have any idea of what they were singing or why. My mother did, and the corner where she sang was truly brightened.

It's that simple courage and that commitment that make life worth living. That's why I ended my song by saying, "This old world is a better place . . . because one time . . . my mama sang a song."

There's no doubt about it. It truly is.

Whisperin' Bill Anderson

Grandfather's Clock

They are not gone who live in the hearts of those they leave behind.

Native American Saying

In the dining room of my grandfather's house stood a massive grandfather clock. Meals in that dining room were a time for four generations to become one. The table was always spread with food from wonderful family recipes all containing love as the main ingredient. And always that grandfather clock stood like a trusted old family friend, watching over the laughter and story swapping and gentle kidding that were a part of our lives.

As a child, the old clock fascinated me. I watched and listened to it during meals. I marveled at how at different times of the day, that clock would chime three times, six times or more, with a wonderful resonant sound that echoed throughout the house. I found the clock comforting. Familiar. Year after year, the clock chimed, a part of my memories, a part of my heart.

Even more wonderful to me was my grandfather's ritual. He meticulously wound that clock with a special key each day. That key was magic to me. It kept our family's magnificent clock ticking and chiming, a part of every holiday and every tradition, as solid as the wood from which it was made. I remember watching as my grandfather took the key from his pocket and opened the hidden door in the massive old clock. He inserted the key and wound—not too much, never overwind, he'd tell me solemnly. Nor too little. He never let that clock wind down and stop. When we grandkids got a little older, he showed us how to open the door to the grandfather clock and let us each take a turn winding the key. I remember the first time I did, I trembled with anticipation. To be part of this family ritual was sacred.

After my beloved grandfather died, it was several days after the funeral before I remembered the clock!

"Mama! The clock! We've let it wind down."

The tears flowed freely when I entered the dining room. The clock stood forlornly quiet. As quiet as the funeral parlor had been. Hushed. The clock even seemed smaller. Not quite as magnificent without my grandfather's special touch. I couldn't bear to look at it.

Sometime later, years later, my grandmother gave me the clock and the key. The old house was quiet. No bowls clanging, no laughter over the dinner table, no ticking or chiming of the clock—all was still. The hands on the clock were frozen, a reminder of time slipping away, stopped at the precise moment when my grandfather had ceased winding it. I took the key in my shaking hand and opened the clock door. All of a sudden, I was a child again, watching my grandfather with his silver-white hair and twinkling blue eyes. He was *there*, winking at me, at the secret of the clock's magic, at the key that held so much power. I stood, lost in the moment for a long time. Then slowly, reverently, I inserted the key and wound the clock. It sprang to life. Tick-tock, tick-tock, life and chimes were breathed into the dining room, into the house and into my heart. In the movement of the hands of the clock, my grandfather lived again.

Kathy Fasig

Angel Unaware

In my unending grief over Robin, something Roy had said kept running through my mind: "She looks like a small-size sleeping angel." I recalled a verse from the thirteenth chapter of Hebrews: *"Be not forgetful to entertain strangers; for thereby some have entertained angels unaware."* You see, our baby girl, Robin Elizabeth Rogers, was born with Down's syndrome. Like sunlight breaking through clouds after a storm of darkness, it all became clear to me. I knew what Robin's life meant and I saw what I had to do. She had come to us from God—an angel—with all her handicaps and frailties to make us aware that his strength is found in weakness. In the two years she had been among us, we had grown close as a family and we had learned how deeply we needed to depend on God. My job was to help deliver that message that had been given us by an angel.

After Robin's death, I grabbed a pen and began to write. I wrote until my hand cramped and could write no more. I looked at the pile of paper on my desk. It was my handwriting, but somehow the words didn't feel like *mine*. I picked up the pen again and tried to write more, but nothing happened. After that initial burst of inspiration, a curtain seemed to fall across my mind and, try as I might, I could not force myself to conjure up the words.

I was obsessed with getting Robin's message onto paper, but didn't know how to do it. One evening during a radio broadcast when I had time away from the microphone, I closed my eyes and sought guidance. In that moment, I knew what the problem was. I was in the way! I was trying so hard to put her message into my words that I was blocking hers. It was so simple! All I had to do was stand aside and let Robin speak for herself. I was not the messenger; I was merely the instrument. From that moment on, the words—her words—flowed onto paper. It turned out to be a short book, but the message was a simple one that didn't need windy elaboration. The story was Robin's—and God's—not mine, and it was for parents and children who needed to understand, so I decided to donate all the royalties to the National Association for Retarded Children. In an introduction to the book that I wrote (in my words), I told readers, "This is what I, her mother, believe she told our Heavenly Father shortly after 8:00 P.M. on August 24, 1952." Her story began:

Oh, Father, it's good to be home again. I thought sometimes that You had forgotten me, Down There. Two years Up Here doesn't seem like much, but on earth it can be a long, long time—and it was long, and often hard, for all of us. When You lifted me up from the earth, just a few minutes ago, it was Sunday, and my Mommy and Daddy were crying, and everything seemed so dark and sad and confused. And all of the sudden it was bright and clear and happy, and I was in Your arms. Was it the same for them Down There, Father? You can put me down, now; I'm perfectly all right, now that I'm rid of that lump of hindering clay. . . .

Robin's story concluded with these words:

> *They're a lot stronger, since they got Our message.*
> *There's a new glory inside them and on everything all*
> *around them, and they've made up their minds to give*
> *it to everybody they meet. The sun's a lot brighter in*
> *Encino, since we stopped off there for a while. And now,*
> *Father, please . . . could I just go out and try my wings?*

I called the manuscript *Angel Unaware*. I soon learned
that the publishing business could be as tough as show
business. The first publisher who read it said they already
had a book about a handicapped child, and didn't want
two. Besides, they informed me, the reading public does
not want to cry. More rejections followed. My faith began
to slip. Why had I been guided to write the book if no one
cared to read it?

We were in New York. I went to Central Park and sat
alone on a bench trying to figure out what to do. I wanted
a sign from God, so I bowed my head to pray. "Please give
me a word," I begged him. "Is it your will that I seek a publisher for Robin's book?" I looked up from my prayer and
saw a little girl standing in the grass looking at me. She
was about six years old. She had slanted eyes, tiny ears,
little square hands and a thick tongue that caused her to
drool. She was a Down's syndrome child, tethered to a
middle-aged woman whose face was furrowed deeply
with the scars of mental anguish. There were hundreds of
office workers strolling in the park at that moment, but I
saw only the mother and child. The little one tried to look
at me, tried hard to focus her weak eyes just as Robin had
done so many times, then walked on. *Oh, thank you, Lord!*
I thought. That girl in the park was the word I had
needed. Now I knew I could persevere until I found a
publisher for Robin's book. I had to let other mothers of

Down's syndrome children know they were not alone. I had to let them know how Robin had blessed our lives.

That afternoon I got a call from Dr. Frank Mead of the Fleming H. Revell Company. He said he wanted to publish *Angel Unaware*. The book was released Easter week, 1953, and it became a bestseller. But I never enjoyed its success as much as I did that autumn at the rodeo in Madison Square Garden.

When Roy and I rode out into the arena, the stands were filled with children, as they always were for our shows. But this year, after the publication of *Angel Unaware*, the audience was different. Among the cheering youngsters were hundreds of retarded boys and girls—Down's syndrome kids—all kinds of kids with disabilities and handicaps—who had been brought to the show by their mothers and fathers. We had never seen them before; in those days parents seldom brought children like that out in public; they kept them in back rooms and closets, as though they weren't human beings. But Robin's book helped change that. Mothers and fathers had come to the rodeo because they wanted us to see their children, and they wanted their children to see us. They told the little ones that Roy and I were their friends. As we circled around, parents proudly held their fragile children in the air so they could wave to us and reach out with their little hands when we passed. The children smiled and laughed when we came close in our glittering cowboy clothes and our prancing horses. Down's syndrome children all share certain features, so I saw Robin's face shining in every one of them. She filled the arena and her love filled my heart. I was blessed.

Dale Evans

A Handful of Blackberries

Just as I began a new job in New York, I had to learn another important job: fatherhood. At the office, we had three new projects in the works, and at home I had a young son who was growing fast and needed me. To say I felt stretched is an understatement. This was never more clear than one Thursday when, for the second time in a week, I was packing for a business trip.

"I know how important your job is," my wife, Ellen, said. "But it would be nice if you could be home more often."

I knew she was right. My son, Luke, was turning three, and I didn't like being away so much either.

"Yesterday," Ellen said, "Luke wandered around the house saying, 'Where is my daddy? Where *is* he?'"

Ellen wanted to discuss this further, but there wasn't time. "Honey, I really have to make this plane," I said. "Let's talk tomorrow when I get back."

In Chicago my meeting ended early, and I suddenly had a couple of hours to kill. So I called on Dan, an old family friend who had retired to the area to be near his grandchildren.

Dan had once farmed in Indiana, where my father was a country doctor. Now, as we sat at his kitchen table, he began to reminisce about what a fine man my dad had been.

"He'd get you well no matter what it took," Dan said. "I don't think there was a soul in that county who didn't love your father."

Then, to my surprise, Dan confided that after he'd recovered from prostate cancer, he had developed a serious depression that he just couldn't shake.

"I didn't care about getting better," he said. "But your daddy got me through it."

His remembrance touched me, and I put my hand on his shoulder. "He cared about his patients a lot," I agreed.

Indeed, I knew how devoted my father was to his patients. But I also knew that his devotion and hard work came with a price—a price that seemed high to his family.

Dad was a tall, lean man whose sky-blue eyes could see straight through anything. But despite his no-nonsense gaze and way of speaking, he was always easy to talk to.

We lived on a farm, not because we were farmers but because many of Dad's patients were. They often paid in livestock instead of cash, so he found a farm to put his fees out to graze.

There was no denying my father's love of hunting, however, and he always kept bird dogs. I would train them until they were ready to hunt. He left that chore to me, he said, because he didn't have the patience. Yet what he did or did not want to do often seemed to hinge on what I might learn from doing it myself. My dad taught me everything. He showed me how to use a handsaw and mark a right angle, for instance—skills that enabled me to cobble together a raft for the pond beyond our meadow. One corner ended up out of line, but Dad helped me launch it without comment on its fault. His best way of helping was to ask questions that allowed me to realize things myself. When I was afraid I'd have to fight a guy at school he asked, "Can you take him?"

"I think so."

"Then you don't have to. Here, stand up and give me a shove."

He made me push him until I nearly knocked him down. "See, you just have to give him an idea of how strong you are. What if you try that and see if he doesn't back off?" I did, and it worked.

That was the kind of help I needed from Dad. But the summer I turned thirteen, he virtually disappeared from my life, and I didn't know what to do.

So many people were sick, and Dad was gone most of the time seeing patients. He was also building a new office and trying to earn enough to pay for an X-ray machine. Often the phone rang while we were at supper and I'd hear him say, "Be right there." Then Mom would cover his plate with a pie tin and put it in the oven to wait.

Many times he'd be gone for an hour or more. Then his car would crunch on the gravel drive, and I'd run downstairs to sit with him while he ate. He'd ask about my day and give me whatever advice I had to have about the farm. But that was about all he had energy for.

As that year went on, I worried about him, and I worried about me. I missed his help. I missed joking around and just being together. *Maybe he doesn't like me as much as he did,* I thought. *Maybe I've done something to disappoint him.* He'd been helping me become a man, and I didn't think I had a prayer of getting that done without his guidance.

The pond beyond the meadow was ringed with reeds and cattails. I liked to fish there. I'd never caught a big one, hooking only sunnies and a few catfish. But big fish were in there. I'd seen them jump, making a glistening turbulence in the mist of early morning. Sometimes the ripples would carry so far they'd reach the shore.

That summer I used to sit on my raft and think of ways to lure my father back. My mother wanted us to take a vacation, but he nixed that because he had so much work.

One day my mother and I stood in the kitchen and talked about him.

"See if you can get him to go fishing," she finally said. "Even just one evening off will help."

The next day I began my campaign to get Dad down to our pond. I planned to make a fire, roast ears of corn and fry up whatever we could catch. The problem was getting my father to change into old clothes and take off a few hours.

Finally, one Friday, I simply bullied him into it. I met his car when he came home and pulled him into the mudroom, where we changed our work clothes.

"We're going fishing," I said. "And that is that."

And we did! As we stood on the pond's edge casting into the fading sunlight, I was still amazed that I'd persuaded him to do it. Soon I went to gather wood for a fire. We hadn't had any luck yet, but we could still roast the corn and talk.

While I worked, I watched him cast into a deep hole near a fallen red oak. "Please let him catch a fish," I whispered to myself. "*Any* fish—just let him catch something."

Almost as if my thought had raised the fish to the lure, a bass struck his line.

"Whoa, boss!" he yelled, and the moss-colored fish took to the air. It looked humongous and put up a good fight as Dad expertly reeled it into his net, then brought it to me by the fire.

"Hey, Dad," I said. "How about that!"

He looked young, happy and proud. I dredged his fish in cornmeal and fried it over the fire. We sat on a stone eating our supper.

"That was some meal," he said when finished. "I don't know when I've liked anything more."

My father made a pot of coffee while I went to the edge of the meadow where the briers were borne down with ripe blackberries. I picked our dessert and carried it back in my baseball cap. We had the berries with our coffee and watched the sun make dazzling colors in the western sky. My father ate slowly, one berry at a time, savoring each. Then out of the blue he began telling me how much he cared about me.

"You know, Son, you're going to be a success in life," he said. "I know that because I never have to ask you to do something twice. But more than that, you're a good kid."

The expression on his face was of such warmth and pride that I felt utterly blessed.

Times like this were all too rare as my father's practice grew ever larger. But whenever I needed to, I'd reach back to that moment by the pond, remembering how good it felt when Dad was with me.

"Yes, sir," Dan said, interrupting my memories. "Your father was some fine man. And his medicine wasn't just pills and shots. He thought a lot about people. He could always understand what someone was going through."

"Yes. Sometimes he did," I said, looking momentarily away.

Then Dan said, "When I was at my worst, I said to him, 'Doc, give me one reason to beat this depression.' And do you know what he said?"

Dan stared across the table until I reestablished eye contact. "He said, 'Blackberries. Think of a handful of blackberries and how wonderful that is. To pick a handful of blackberries, sit down with someone you love very much and eat them. Think of that and tell me life's not worth the fight. You have a wonderful wife and three fine kids. Take some time with them. It's family we live for— not just ourselves.'

"That's what he said, and I've never forgotten it," Dan finished. "I think it saved my life."

My hands were quivering. All I could do was stare back at him. I felt so many emotions that I could muster not one word.

On the plane home, I closed my eyes and thought about me and my dad. I knew what that day by the pond had meant to me. But I had never known what it meant to him. Now, in my mind's eye, I saw him standing at the edge of the water, the bass on his line, so full of joy. *How wide the ripples spread*, I thought. *How far they reach.*

Suddenly I found myself staring out the airplane window, hoping that the flight would get in on time. I planned to be home before dark for a change—to play in the yard with my son in the fading light of day.

W. W. Meade

Reprinted by permission of Dave Carpenter. ©1998 Dave Carpenter.

Fishing with Granddaddy

It's five o'clock in the morning and he's waking me up. But it's hard. It's summertime, I'm ten years old, and this is supposed to be vacation. The days of rest and relaxation. Then my eyes squint open. I can barely see his face, lined and ancient. But I'm happy. Very happy. Today my granddaddy and I are going fishing.

He creeps into the kitchen while I put on the clothes I selected the night before. Blue jeans, but not good ones; instead the jeans I hoped would later that day bear the mud stains and the fish smell. It almost seemed like a rule. The more disgusting the clothes, the better the day had been. If Mom made me undress on the porch before I even dared enter her clean house, I knew it had been a wonderful day indeed.

The shirt couldn't be white. Granddaddy said it spooked the fish, so I'm wearing my old blue football jersey.

I find my way into the kitchen. He had made me a cup of coffee. Lots of sugar and lots of cream. I can't imagine anyone drinking the stuff any other way. *I bet none of my friends are drinking coffee this morning. I bet they won't drink coffee for another eight or ten years.* I watch as he finishes loading up the cooler. There are no wasted movements. This is a task he has perfected over the years. You do something a million times, you learn to get it right.

The menu rarely changes. A thermos of ice water. Four Coca-Colas in the little bottles. A few packs of peanut butter crackers and two ham sandwiches. White bread. Mustard and mayonnaise.

He tells me to get my coat. It's always cold before the sun comes up. Even in July. I grab my zip-up sweatshirt with the hood. I wish I had a jacket like his: a blue jean jacket with a red and black flannel lining. The jacket bears many miles, and they're not highway miles. I've never seen another one quite like it. He and the jacket seem to belong together. They fit each other.

Granddaddy unlocks the camper top and slides the cooler into the back along with the rest of the gear we loaded the night before. Everything has its place. The cooler goes in back of his tackle box, but in front of the trolling motor battery. I always insist on carrying the battery to prove I am a worthy fishing companion. Man, is it heavy! But I will never say so out loud even though I'm sure my labored stagger must give it away. I don't think I've ever picked up that battery without a warning not to spill acid on myself. Through all the years I've never seen one drop of anything come out of that battery, but I fear it nonetheless. Granddaddy's warning always makes it sound like the acid will burn a hole clear through my leg before I can even get my pants off. Very scary stuff.

He is a very methodical driver. I'm not sure of very many things in life, but I would be willing to bet everything I own, Ted Williams model baseball glove included, that he has never gotten a speeding ticket. Sometimes I have to glance down to make sure he's actually mashing the gas. I assume that he is because the black work shoe is resting on the pedal. Black work shoes with white socks. If he has another combination, I've never seen it.

Granddaddy is a man of few fashion surprises. I find the consistency to be comforting.

Our trips are never cluttered with chitchat. When he talks it is to brag about having the fastest radio in Georgia. He turns it on and off twice to back up his words. I'm confident that they don't hold contests to determine such things, but I still can't imagine anyone capable of proving him wrong.

I can't remember riding with Granddaddy where he did not find at least one opportunity to pull the same corny joke on me. He points down the road and says, "There's your name on a sign. 'Old Stopper Head.'" Of course the sign really reads "Stop Ahead," but it never fails to make the two of us laugh. It's just one more reason I know the old man likes me.

We have a few regular fishing holes. Most of them are small ponds located on the property of different farmers he has met over the years. He always stops at the house to confirm that it is okay that we fish. I am required to go with him and to say "Thank you for letting us fish." We are always extra careful to lock gates and never leave a mess.

When we reach our fishing spot, we unload the gear in the same fashion we loaded it: meticulously and painstakingly slow. But I'm always in a hurry. I worry that the fish will stop biting at any moment. Time is of the essence.

We always put the tackle boxes and the rods and reels into the boat last. Granddaddy's tackle box is roughly the size of a small barn. I'm sure it carries one of everything ever designed to entice a fish. Sometimes when the fish aren't biting I entertain myself just looking through it. I'm always asking what different things are, and he usually explains, and follows with a grand story of a fish that fell victim to its charm.

My tackle box, on the other hand, is about the size of a shoe box. I have painted my name and a picture of a bass jumping out of the water on top of it. It contains mostly the cherished discards from his box. There are a few lures I have bought myself—all replicas of the ones he holds in highest regard. Unfortunately, they never seem to catch nearly as many fish as his lures do.

I am always amazed at the ease and accuracy with which he casts. Granddaddy will always say something like, "Well, if I hadn't of throwed right there I never would have caught this one." Then with the flick of his wrist he sends his lure sailing through the air and it comes to rest inches from a semisubmerged log that should have a sign painted on it that reads "Home of a Monster Bass." I try to emulate his technique, but I spend lots of my fishing time trying to pull my lure out of the limb in which it is firmly anchored.

He always catches more fish than I do. Usually about fifteen to my one. *How can he be so lucky every single time?* When he hooks one, he really seems to enjoy reeling it in. As he cranks, he gives a play-by-play commentary complete with estimates about the fish's size, where he hit it, and guesses about what the scoundrel might do to avoid eventually joining us in the boat.

On the other hand, when I get lucky enough to hook one, I retrieve it with all the calmness of Barney Fife making an arrest. There is no savoring the moment. I reel so fast and pull so hard that I have been known to make a fish go airborne. You should see the look on a fish's face when he breaks the water, sails over the boat and resubmerges on the other side. "He looks like a pretty good one," I hear my granddaddy chuckle. I ignore him, because this is no time for jokes. If I don't get this thing into the boat, then I have no proof that I actually caught one. *After all, who's going to believe a fisherman?*

It is then as I'm staring at him that I am always filled with a little pity for the fish. Not because he started the day in a cool lake playing fish games with his friends and will end it wearing a cornmeal jacket in the bottom of a frying pan. I feel pity because he fell to me instead of the old man.

We conclude much the way we started, only in reverse order. We are careful to leave the place as we found it. Granddaddy says, "That's how you get to come back." We pick up trash and lock gates. We always stop back by the house and thank the folks for letting us fish on their place. Granddaddy always offers them our fish, while I silently pray that if they do take some, mine won't be in that number. Thankfully, that has never happened.

We return home to the ceremonial showing off of the catch. Granddaddy is much more low key and humble in his approach than I am in mine. By that I mean that he doesn't leap from the truck, grab the stringer and go running through the house screaming, "Look what I caught! Look what I caught!" Of course he is also spared the lecture from my mom about how hard it is to get the smell of dripping fish out of the living-room rug.

Finally, I am required to help Granddaddy clean the fish, though it is a job I don't mind. The combination of scales and entrails is enough to make the football jersey truly disgusting. I wear the mess like a medal. It is a proud moment.

Job complete, we head back into the house. Already I am growing excited and planning our next trip, the trip that may net one of us that fish of a lifetime. Granddaddy knows what I'm thinking. He musses my hair and smiles. I hope I can go fishing with him forever.

Jeff Foxworthy

The Button Jar

I wish I had known my grandparents when they were young. By the time I was old enough to be interested in them as people, they were very elderly. My grandfather always wore dark blue or brown overalls and was a tobacco farmer who also worked in the coal mines. My grandmother was a housewife and mother. Her daily chores included cooking, cleaning and feeding the farm hands, who consisted of many friends and cousins who helped my grandfather.

When I was a child, my parents would take my sister and me to my grandparents' farm for the weekend. During one of these visits, we discovered the Button Jar. It was a typical winter day in Kentucky, cold and drizzling just enough rain that our mother wouldn't let us go outside. We hadn't brought any toys with us, thinking that we were going to explore the farm all weekend, and we were disgruntled and gloomy at the prospect of staying inside.

Trying to entertain ourselves, we picked at the leftover cornbread Mamaw had left on the kitchen table. In the back room, we spit on the little coal stove, watching the spittle bounce and spew until it evaporated. Bored, we lay down on the thick quilts on the iron bed where we slept, and imagined pictures out of the water spots on the sagging ceiling. We played Riddle-Mer-Riddle-Mer-Riddle-Merie until we couldn't stand it anymore. I had that lonesome, empty feeling that often comes with childhood boredom, and I was determined that we do something.

My sister and I looked at each other and knowingly, without saying a word, decided to eavesdrop on the adults. We wandered into the living room and listened to the men sitting around the potbellied stove, telling hunting and fishing stories. Bored with that, we went into the kitchen to listen to the women talk about the task of raising children and what they were preparing for supper that night. This bored us too. Mamaw noticed we were fidgeting and said, "You girls come here a minute."

She led us into her bedroom and reached for a large glass jar that sat on top of the old mahogany chifforobe. The jar was full of every sort of button you could imagine!

Delighted, we climbed up onto her high four-poster bed and watched as she lovingly poured out all the red, blue, yellow and purple—every color—buttons onto the chenille bedspread. She smiled and said, "Maybe you'd like to play with these for a while."

"Yes!" we cried in unison.

We began by trying to count the buttons, but there were hundreds and we always lost count. That's when we actually looked closely at the buttons. At first glance, we thought that they were made of every color imaginable, but when we looked more closely, we realized what a real treasure we had. One that caught our eyes was a gold metal button, covered with sparkling rhinestones. We turned it over in our hands and marveled at its beauty, wondering how our plain country grandmother had ever come by such a valuable jewel. We carefully sorted out other unique buttons. There were silver buttons, shaped like tiny love knots and large gold buttons set with tiny red, blue, green and gold rhinestones. And although we had never seen silk before, we were quite sure that the fabric-covered buttons were made of silk. As we sorted the buttons, I noticed a tiny clipping of black velvet fabric and thread still attached to a glittering rhinestone button. I looked over at my sister in awe and whispered, "These buttons are off real clothes! Just imagine the kind of dress Mamaw must have had with this button!"

"I'll bet it was a long black velvet dress that she wore to a big dance or party!" my sister said.

We imagined how Mamaw must have looked when she was the mayor's daughter and clearly the prettiest girl in town. We saw before us the life of a popular young socialite who, at age fifteen, had traded that life for marriage.

We found large, chunky black buttons cut from some old coat of my grandfather's, and we pictured him climbing down into the cold, dusty coal mines. We envisioned him wearing this coat at night, with his miner's helmet and carbide lantern so he could see to plow the garden and fields. Inlaid anchors adorned a large pair of jacket buttons that we thought Grandpa must have worn during his Navy days while traveling the world.

We spent hours that day pretending, imagining and creating our own stories about our grandparents. We began to see them as they were when they were young adults just beginning in life, as real people, and not just elderly grandparents. These were people who had loved and served life well.

From that day on, every time we were housebound, we shyly asked Mamaw if she'd get down the Button Jar for us. She always smiled knowingly, stopped kneading her biscuits or shelling beans, and got it for us.

My grandmother died soon after I was grown and married, and I regret that I never even thought to tell her about the valuable gift she had given me and my sister when we were children, but I'm sure she knew.

The buttons illustrated that we were part of a continuing story—a story larger than ourselves. Buttons are inexpensive little items, made of plastic or metal, and they are used to hold things together. Mamaw's buttons were fasteners, too, but they did much more than hold clothes together. . . . They held our family together with stories from the past and present. They formed a lasting legacy for our current family and for generations to come, one that continues to warm my heart and nourish my soul.

Susan Wells Pardue

My Father's Hands

Tenderness and kindness are not signs of weakness, but manifestations of strength.

Kahlil Gibran

As my father's devoted and only daughter, I noticed things about him my two brothers never mentioned or may have taken for granted. Two things in particular made Daddy more wonderful, interesting and capable than all the other fathers I'd ever seen or heard of— Daddy's large, sensitive hands. How wonderfully warm they were when I placed mine in his to be rubbed warm on cold winter days. Daddy's hands had endless capabilities, from braiding my pigtails or successfully retrieving a kite from the topmost branches of a tree, to washing my little brother's diapers by hand when we couldn't afford a washing machine. Whatever the job or situation, his tireless hands actively carried it out.

When he was a child, the eldest of seven children, Daddy went to work in order to help support his family. His own father's failing health made it necessary for Daddy to drop out of school. He never complained about being a provider at such a young age. Perhaps that is where his hands found their direction.

Daddy had long, nimble fingers that could thread the smallest needle in order to mend the hem in my dress or sew on a missing button. They could carefully trim the nails of tiny fingers and toes, remove splinters, bandage skinned knees, and, unlike Mama, Daddy could tie straight sashes on my party dresses. Those same agile fingers had a magical way of strumming guitar strings, making my nursery tunes the most beautiful music I ever heard.

Daddy's inventive hands were also strong and useful, wonderfully tanned from working in the sun, and a bit callused. There was no unfamiliar territory to Daddy's hands. They could whip up a delicious and colorful meal in minutes (pancakes were his specialty and favorite). I loved to watch in wonder as his skillful hands worked.

Daddy's hands conveyed a message as they tenderly stroked a fevered brow or mended a broken doll. They seemed to speak, to understand unspoken pain and emotional hurt when I found no way to vocalize this. Daddy's hands soothed and sympathized through their touch as no words could.

Yes, these were the hands of my father. Hands with the knowledge of household repairs and heavy equipment that tenderly, untiringly cared for his children and my mother through her many long illnesses right up until her death with the soothing expertise of nurse and husband. Somehow, during those times when I was sick, it wasn't so bad. Daddy would take a small blanket, warm it in front of the fireplace and wrap it around my small, cold feet with hands of love. Comfortably settled in his lap, it was apparent even then that no mother's hands could have done better. How comfortable to be "all snuggled in," sensing that everything would be all right!

Memories of the old, familiar railroad songs Daddy sang, as his reassuring hands patted me in time to the tune, linger still. Peacefully I sucked my thumb, nestled contented, loved and secure against the rhythm of Daddy's heartbeat while the old rocking chair creaked back and forth. At these times, Daddy did not mention my thumb sucking. With my other hand, I would hold one of Daddy's large hands studying the contours, tracing the lines, caressing the rough spots, now and then encircling my entire hand around one of his warm fingers with pride. Daddy's nails were always trimmed, although he had a permanent split that made a funny design in his left thumbnail. This, too, was special and endeared him to me more because he was building my dollhouse when he acquired the injury.

My father's hands were perfect in my little-girl eyes. They had the strength and power to move mountains. They made the impossible possible!

Years later, in a small hospital room as Daddy lay near death, too weak to speak out loud, I sat tearfully at his bedside. But, holding his hands, those delightful, formative, important years of shared experiences paraded before me in fond and vivid reminiscence. I smiled, recalling special moments as I proudly held those same wonderful hands in mine, seeking out and feeling once again every crevice and line, every callus and scar. I marveled at the many years these magnificent, dedicated, untiring hands had devoted to his family. What an experience of love they had brought. I lifted them, placing the tired, now pale hands against my face, reveling in how warm they were even now just as in my cherished yesterdays. I kissed each brown spot, reminders of his eighty-three years, but I did not see these brown places as "age spots." To me they were beauty marks instead, representing a job well done. I could no longer hold back the tears filling my eyes.

For a brief moment, Daddy roused and opened his eyes as if he wanted to speak. I leaned over close to hear his whisper. With a faint, concerned smile of love, his trembling fingers reached up to gently trace my brow, stopping momentarily to wipe away the tears now glistening on the cheeks of his "little girl." And time stood still. Then Daddy closed his eyes and, sighing one final breath, slipped quietly away.

As I looked down fondly at the precious, motionless hands of my dear father, I knew one thing for sure then, and I am even more sure of it now: No mother's hands, in all the world, were ever more endearing or more beautiful than the hands of my father.

Floanne Kersh

Bird Heaven

We shall all meet in heaven.

Last Words of Andrew Jackson

While I was standing at the kitchen window, five-year-old Spencer, my oldest son, ran into the house screaming, "We need a doctor out here! We need a doctor! Hurry, Mom!!"

"What's wrong?" I asked.

Spencer anxiously told me he had found a dead bird that needed a doctor.

Dutifully, I grabbed a small plastic bag from the pantry and took Spencer's hand—after all, that's the sort of thing mother's do! While my son led me out the door and toward the bird, I explained that if the creature was indeed dead, a doctor could not help. When we arrived at the accident scene, it was obvious that the baby bird was dead. Spencer and I could see the nest high up in the tree. My son and I discussed the probable age of the baby bird, its inability to fly well, and exactly how the fall had caused its death.

"I bet his mommy and daddy really miss him," Spencer observed. I reached for my boy's hand and tried to ease his sadness by saying I was sure they did, but that they would be okay because the little bird had gone to Heaven to be with God and PoPo (my deceased grandfather). I assured Spencer that the bird's mommy and daddy knew their little one would be cared for and loved. I told Spencer that PoPo loved little birds, and I was sure he was in Heaven holding and playing with the baby bird right then. I picked up the little creature's body, slipped it into my plastic bag and gently placed the bird in the trash can. Nothing else was said about the matter for the rest of the day. Spencer went right back to playing as if he had never been interrupted, and I returned to my work in the kitchen.

At breakfast the next morning, Spencer sadly explained to his father that he had found a baby bird the day before that had fallen from its nest.

"It was dead, Daddy!"

Trying to lift Spencer's spirits and remind him that the little bird was really okay, I asked our son to tell Daddy where the baby bird was. Spencer, looking solemn-faced at his dad, stated, "In the trash can with Mama's grand-daddy, PoPo."

Merilyn Gilliam

My Angelique

In the twenty years that I've spent on the road as a tour manager and bodyguard for some of the top bands in rock and pop music, I've seen and experienced some incredible things. I've watched the sun rise like glistening gold dust on the beaches of Maui. Seated comfortably in a Lear jet, I have awakened to see the majestic Swiss Alps at dawn over three different European countries. I've sped across Japan in the cabin of a bullet train. I've stared at both solar and lunar eclipses. I've marveled at the brilliant northern lights beaming over the Laurentian Mountains of Canada. I've witnessed mud slides, fires, earthquakes and floods as well as snowstorms that lasted over forty days and nights. I thought I had experienced it all—but I was wrong. Each and every one of these incredible and awesome experiences pales in comparison with the humbling *wonder* I felt following the birth of my daughter, Angelique Gabrielle.

The exhilaration that took possession of me the day she was born was total; I had to be there for *everything*. Seated by my wife's side, I was Ellen's coaching, consoling husband during her hours of labor. Later, when the actual delivery began, I turned into an unstoppable paparazzo. I took dozens of pictures that no one later cared to see.

I had doctors photograph me holding my Angelique while her umbilical cord was still attached. After taking Ellen's hands in mine and reminding her how very much I loved her, I took pictures of my long-suffering wife looking exhausted and totally disinterested following her ordeal. I took pictures of the doctors. While I gazed upon my incredibly pink, incredibly tiny new daughter as she rested in my hands, I felt I was looking into the Face of Creation. How could I have known what it would be like to love anyone so intensely?

The year my daughter was born, I ended my career as a tour manager. I swore I would never go back on the road again. But when Angelique was two, I was given the opportunity to compile *Chicken Soup for the Country Soul.* Unfortunately, the only method I could think of for obtaining stories from touring musicians was to do the one thing I'd promised I wouldn't do—go back on the road. That was one of the hardest decisions I've ever made. Fortunately, after a year, I was able to move my wife and daughter to Nashville to be with me.

One Nashville night while I was up late writing at the kitchen table, I heard a soft and gentle voice at my side. Angelique, then three years old, tugged on my shirtsleeve and said, "Daddy, it's dark in my bedroom. Will you come and stay with me so I can get to sleep?" Is it any wonder that her bedtime has always been the most precious hour of the day for me?

"Sure, Honey," I replied, pulling my six-foot-four, three-hundred-pound frame up from my chair. I took her little hand in mine and accompanied her quietly down the hall. When we reached her bedroom, we knelt in prayer before I tucked Angelique in under the covers and sat by her side. I told her to close her eyes and promised to stay until she fell asleep. I vowed I wouldn't let any harm come to her while the sandman visited her dreams. In the soft glow of the night-light, I watched as her tiny fingers pulled the tattered security blanket up to her chin and my baby girl closed her eyes. Without warning, I was overcome by a wave of emotion and my heart split open. Quietly, unashamed, I let soft, gentle tears flow from my eyes. I couldn't believe how much I loved her. On that night, and on many other nights since, I've had no difficulty finding the words to let my precious Angelique know how much her daddy loves her.

My Angelique

In the midnight hour, like a cherub doll,
Soft cheeks so tender, wonder on her brow,
Like a statue baby, skin as white as snow,
Long hair of amber, her face is all aglow.

I've heard angels laughing, I've heard them cry,
I've seen angels dancing, in her daddy's eye.
Like a ray of sunshine, in a world so bleak,
She could smile a sunrise, My Angelique.

Only three years old, with a tender soul,
She holds life's answers, in her heart of gold.
Buttons, bows and dresses, my baby doll so sweet,
She redefined my life now, My Angelique.

I've heard angels laughing, I've heard them cry,
I've seen angels dancing, in her daddy's eye.
Like a ray of sunshine, in a world so bleak,
She could smile a sunrise, My Angelique.

Ron Camacho

3

THE POWER
OF FAITH

Count your blessings, instead of your crosses.
Count your gains, instead of your losses.
Count the yes's, instead of the no's.
Count your friends, instead of your foes.
Count your full years, instead of your lean.
Count your health, instead of your wealth,
And count on God, instead of yourself.

Source Unknown

Virtuous Woman

Once the dreams began, they never stopped, but once they did I wished they would start up again. They were always the same—an explosion, fires burning, an army tank overturned and my son Jimmy's body lying on the ground. Someone was taking his rings and watch off, and I would wake up crying, saying his name over and over: "Jimmy . . . Jimmy." I was afraid to close my eyes, even to take a nap. The dreams kept coming and they were so real.

The strange thing was, Jimmy was still in basic training at Fort Knox, Kentucky. He didn't know about the dreams, and wouldn't. I was afraid to give voice to them to anyone. Finally, from sheer exhaustion, I collapsed and was hospitalized. Four days later I awoke to find Jimmy sitting by my bed. It seemed, in my unconscious state I had repeatedly called his name. The doctor had contacted him and Jimmy got a ten-day leave. I told him it was just exhaustion, but the worried look on his face made me vow to myself that this would never happen again. I assured him of that. The dreams were never mentioned. I was to see him two more times.

After Fort Knox Jimmy was sent to Fort Polk, Louisiana, for advanced infantry training (AIT) where he received word he was being sent to Vietnam, but would be coming home for three weeks before going. Corky, my middle son, who had volunteered two months after Jimmy was drafted, and would also be going to Vietnam, was at that time stationed at Fort Sill, Oklahoma. On Jimmy's leave, Corky, my youngest son David, and I went there so we could all be together for four days.

After boarding the plane to come home, Jimmy looked out the window at Corky still standing at the gate and said, "That's the last time I'll see Corky."

I said "Please don't say that." But he just said, "It's true, Mom," and never spoke another word all the way home.

After arriving back in Nashville, I had to take David back to the private school he was attending, but waited as long as possible so he and Jimmy could spend time together. As I headed David for the car, Jimmy said, "That's the last time I'll see David."

He saw the look on my face and said, "It's true, Mom," and went back into the house.

The next morning I awoke to the sound of the riding lawn mower. Looking out the window, I saw Jimmy in cut off Levi's and tennis shoes mowing the backyard. I took him some lemonade and said, "You don't have to mow the lawn."

He looked around at the house, the yard, at me and his car sitting in the driveway, everything, then said, "I like to mow this yard, and who knows, it may be the last time."

The next day, at three in the morning on American Airlines, he left for Oakland, California. Before boarding the plane he hugged me and said, "Promise me you'll always sing 'Where No One Stands Alone' for me." I promised.

Three days later he was on his way to Vietnam. At midnight that night the phone rang. The operator said, "I have a collect call from Wake Island. Will you accept the

call?" Practically screaming, I said, "Yes!" I will never forget these words. "Mom," he said, "I know it's a long ways
and costs a lot of money, but I just had to hear your voice
one more time." We both said "I love you," then he was
gone. Sleep was a long time coming.

The nightmares continued. Corky came home on leave
before he was to go to Vietnam. One day as I was writing
Jimmy a letter, it turned into what I guess you would call
a poem. The beginning line was, "My son, my son, I pray
that you'll come home to me my son, my son." Finishing
the whole letter, I read it to Corky. He said I should put
it to music and send it to Jimmy. "He would be so proud,"
he said. My producer, Owen Bradley, and my friend and
coworker, Bill Anderson, agreed.

Two weeks later I went into the studio but couldn't
sing without crying. Owen said, "Jan, it's just another
song."

"No, Owen," I said, "It's my son's life." Gently, he said,
"If you can get through it one time, we'll take it." I did. In
my next letter to Jimmy I told him to expect a small package, but didn't tell him it was a tape of the song. I wanted
it to be a surprise. "My Son" was released two weeks
later. I tried to sing it in concerts, but the words couldn't
get past the lump in my throat. Corky left for Vietnam
exactly two months at the exact hour and minute after
Jimmy left; the twentieth of August.

October the twentieth I went to Atlanta, where I
worked the next week. Worked and cried. I called my
attorney, who was in the National Guard, and asked him
to please check on the boys. His answer was, "Jan, they're
all right or you would know." I told him that was the
problem. . . . I did know. At the end of the engagement I
returned home and did not leave my house.

Wednesday, October 29, I asked a friend how I would
be notified if anything happened to my sons. I was told

that two uniformed officers would come to my door. When I awoke Thursday morning I realized I had not had the dream. I showered and dressed in a pair of blue jeans and a light blue shirt, but no shoes. Ordinarily I would then put on makeup, but that morning I knew there was no use. My friend Jeannie Bare called and asked if I was all right. It was obvious she was crying. When I asked what was wrong, she said, "Oh, it can wait. I'll call you back." After that it was as if I was in a trance moving in slow motion. Ordinarily I would have turned on the *Today Show*, but not that morning. The phone rang again. It was my hairdresser asking me to please open the door because "they" had been ringing the bell for half an hour. I had not heard the doorbell or anyone knocking. "Who are 'they'?" I asked and hung up the phone. But I knew. I don't remember going downstairs.

When I opened the door, I saw two uniformed officers and my son David, who rushed forward and grabbed me as I began backing up, screaming, "No! No!"

But David, sobbing, told me the news: "Mom ... Jimmy's dead." Over my screams I heard one of the officers say, "Mrs. Howard, we regret to inform you your son is dead." That's the last thing I remember, but I understand David, all one hundred and fifteen pounds of him, carried me upstairs to my bedroom. Five days later the plane arrived carrying Jimmy's body, escorted by my son Corky.

Though I prayed to die, I knew I had to live for David and Corky. But I had one request: "When Jimmy's letter comes, I want it." They told me there would be no more letters, but I was adamant there would be. Jimmy's funeral was on Tuesday and his letter arrived on Saturday. In it, he gave me instructions like "Don't get behind in your washing and ironing; you know that's your downfall. And promise you'll take a vacation now and then. You know you're not made of iron." He also said, "I know Christmas will be there before you know it. Please don't be sad because I won't be there in person. Remember I'll always be with you in spirit."

Thirty days later I still had not left my bedroom and had done nothing but cry and read and reread Jimmy's last letter. It was the first time I had been alone. Again, I was reading his letter just to see his handwriting. Suddenly he was beside me on the bed, dressed in his stay-pressed pants, V-neck sweater and open-neck shirt, the clothes he usually wore to school. He looked so sad. "Mom," he said, "I've been trying to get through to you, but I can't. Read the last chapter before the book of Ecclesiastes." I screamed, "Jimmy!" and reached to touch him, but he was gone.

At that moment Corky walked in. I told him Jimmy had been there. He said, "Now, Mom . . ." But I assured him I wasn't crazy and then told him what Jimmy had said to me. Corky got the Bible and turned to the last chapter of Proverbs. It told about Lemuel, King of Massa, and how his mother taught him advice about life. It went on to tell about the rareness of a capable, intelligent and virtuous woman. "She is far more precious than fine jewels. . . . her children rise up and call her blessed. . . . many daughters have done virtuously, nobly and well, but you excel them all." I knew Jimmy had spoken to me through those words. He knew the Bible, but except for Matthew, Mark, Luke and John, I didn't. I couldn't have told you there was a book of Ecclesiastes in the Bible and he knew that. And he knew Corky would know.

Jimmy could never stand to see me cry or hurt in any way and he knew I was literally grieving myself to death. In my heart I believe that God allowed him to return for just those few seconds to share words that would help me to live.

When my sons went to Vietnam, I had prayed so hard for their safe return. But when Jimmy was killed, I turned away. One minute I would say I didn't want to hear God's name, but in the next I'd be praying for strength. . . . which, through His Grace, I received. The first time I went back to church, I was late and the minister was already into his sermon. . . . The text that day was the last chapter of Proverbs.

Thank you, Lord.

Jan Howard

Deck of Cards

It was during the Vietnam conflict when a bunch of soldiers had been on a long hike. They arrived in a town called Saigon, and the next day being Sunday, several of the boys went to church. After the chaplain read the prayer, the text was taken out. Those of the boys that had prayer books took them out; but one boy had a deck of cards, so he spread them out.

The sergeant in charge of the boys saw the cards, and after the service the soldier was taken prisoner and brought before the provost marshal. The marshal asked, "Sergeant, why have you brought this man here?"

"For playing cards in church, sir."

"And what do you have to say for yourself, son?"

"Much, sir," the soldier replied.

The marshal said, "I hope so. If not, I shall punish you severely."

"You see, I've been on the march for six days and I had neither a Bible or a prayer book; but I hope to satisfy you with the purity of my intentions.

"You see, when I look at the ace, it reminds me that there is one God. When I see the deuce, it reminds me that the Bible is divided into two parts—the Old and

New Testaments. And when I see the three, I think of the Father, Son and the Holy Ghost. When I see the four, I think of the four evangelists who preached the gospel; that was Matthew, Mark, Luke and John. And when I see the five, it reminds me of the five wise virgins who trimmed their lamps. There was ten of them—five were wise and were saved; five were foolish and they were shut out. When I see the six, it reminds me that in six days, God made heaven and earth. And when I see the seven, it reminds me that on the seventh day God rests. When I see the eight, I think of the eight righteous persons God saved when he destroyed the earth. There was Noah and his wife, their three sons and three wives. And when I see the nine, I think of the leper our Savior cleansed. When I think of ten, I think of ten heavenly saints, and when I see the king, it reminds me again that there is but one King of Heaven. And when I think of the queen, I think of the blessed Virgin Mary, who is Queen of Heaven, and the jack reminds me of the devil.

"When I count the number of spots on the deck, I find 365—the number of days in the year. There are fifty-two cards—the number of weeks in the year. There are thirteen tricks—the number of weeks in a quarter. There are four suits—the number of weeks in a month. There are twelve picture cards—the number of months in a year.

"So you see, sir, my deck of cards served me as a Bible, almanac and prayer book."

Friends, this story is true. . . . because my son was that soldier.

T. Texas Tyler

Promises Kept

Events that would forever change the lives of two young brothers started when John was twelve and Malcolm was eleven. At the time, they were visiting their grandmother's farm in Goodlettsville, Tennessee. Though the boys were supposed to go to church that morning, they had decided to go crow hunting instead, so they stayed home with their aunt and uncle.

As the boys prepared to go hunting, they loaded the rifle, set it in a corner of the living room and filled their canteens. Because they weren't allowed to go after crows 'til their aunt and uncle left for church, the boys got to feeling their oats and started roughhousing. Before long, Malcolm—who had forgotten that the gun was loaded— picked it up and began pointing it around the room. John shouted, "Don't point that thing at me—it's loaded!"

"No, it's not," Malcolm said as he squeezed the trigger.

But it was. The rifle went off and a bullet hit John in the side of the head, penetrating several inches into his brain. The saving grace was that he had on earmuffs fitted with a thin steel band that clamped the muffs to his head. That metal band split the .22 cartridge into several pieces so the bullet didn't go as deep as it would have if it had been whole. Yet the fragments crushed the entire side of John's skull and went into the brain.

Seconds after the shot rang out, John hit the floor yelling, "You shot me!" He fell with his head next to the bed so all that could be seen was blood trickling onto the rug. Malcolm thought for sure that his brother was going to die. Their aunt heard the shot and came running. She knelt down, took a close look at John, got up and ran out into the yard, where her husband was fixing to go to church. They put John into their car and took him over to the funeral home for transfer to an ambulance. From the funeral home, the boys' aunt and uncle went with the ambulance to the hospital. All this time, Malcolm was left alone at the house. That was the first time he had ever prayed in earnest.

"Dear Lord," he said, "Let my brother live. Let him live, and I'll become a preacher." Up until that moment, he had never even *thought* of being a preacher!

On the way to the hospital, John began praying in earnest also. Over and over again, as he felt the blood oozing from his head, he said, "Dear Lord, let me live and I'll become a doctor."

When John got to St. Thomas Hospital, the brain surgeon told his parents, who had arrived by that time, that the damage was severe enough that, while the boy might live, he would probably be a vegetable—unable to walk, or talk, or do anything for himself for the rest of his life.

Later on when Malcolm got to the hospital, he was told the same awful news about his brother. Overcome with remorse, Malcolm was left alone in a small room with only his thoughts for company. That was when the Lord spoke to him. (It was the first and last time he ever had this experience in his entire life.) God told him, "John is going to be alright. Don't worry about it."

It wasn't long at all before John got strong enough to go back home—but he still couldn't talk. By then it was summer. The house didn't have air conditioning, so the windows were kept open most of the time. One afternoon, the family was sitting in the kitchen, not far from John's room, when all of a sudden they heard someone going, "Ugh, ugh." They rushed into the bedroom and discovered that a wasp had gotten under John's blanket. It was then that John decided he would talk.

Doc McClure thought John's recovery was such a miracle that he got doctors from all over the area to come and look at the boy and check his X rays to confirm this miraculous recovery.

Did the boys keep their promises to God? While Malcolm *did* become a preacher, the fact is he tried everything he could to get out of it.

After high school, he attended Martin College. He was sitting in his dormitory room one Friday evening when the district superintendent walked in and said, "Someone told me you want to be a preacher; is that right?"

Now Malcolm didn't remember telling *anybody* he wanted to be a preacher—in fact, he was *certain* he hadn't breathed a word to anyone! "Yeah . . . yeah, I guess that would be nice," was his less than enthusiastic response.

"Well, that's *great* because we got a little circuit down here in Wayne County, Tennessee, that doesn't have a preacher. . . . They will be looking for you this Sunday."

As it turned out, those Wayne County folks may not have wanted a preacher. But then, Malcolm was the nearest thing to *nothing* they could have found. So they sent him to the largest circuit in the state, where he started pastoring six churches. In 1957, Malcolm got his license to preach, later attended Vanderbilt Seminary and has enjoyed pastoring ever since.

Now what about John, his brother? He not only recovered, he became an all-'round athlete. He played football, basketball, track and more. He graduated as valedictorian of his high school class with the highest grade point average in Marshall County, Tennessee—98.9. After that, John entered the Sewanee University, where he finished his premed studies in three years. He later became a board-certified radiologist and went on to achieve the rank of colonel in the U.S. Air Force. Today, John is a partner of the Rush Medical Clinic in Meridian, Mississippi.

Now you may be wondering how I've come to know so much about these two boys. That's not hard to explain—*Dr. John Patton is my brother.*

Reverend Malcolm Patton

Too Broken to Be Fixed

The people in my family believed if something went
wrong, it was always someone else's fault. I readily
picked up this attitude and ran with it. Actually, when
you think about it, it's not a bad plan. I was not responsible for any of my failures; they were always someone
else's fault. Holding on to this thought, I was able to feel
anger toward the "responsible parties," rather than feeling inadequate myself.

Of course, one of the side effects of this attitude is
simple: You never get very far in life. You never learn from
your mistakes because, after all, they weren't your mistakes.
Or perhaps the "responsible parties" hurt you on purpose,
so the anger builds over the years to the point where the
smoldering rage is, at best, kept just under the surface.

Finally you ask yourself the question, Why are so many
people out to get me? and the only logical answer is that
even God hates you. So if you were like me, you return
the favor and hate God right back. My belief that God
hated me grew as the years passed, and I perceived each
setback as further evidence that my belief was correct. I
had heard it said that God works through people. Seeing
the number of people out to get me, I knew this was true.

Even as a child, I learned to fight back, so it is not surprising that as an adult, I gradually fell deeper and deeper into a violent lifestyle. I became very good at hurting people, yet strangely, I always hated myself for it afterward, especially if I hurt someone I cared about. Gradually I learned to stay away from anyone that I cared about, and I became a loner. I knew that all I could do with any consistency was hurt people, so I tried to keep it down to hurting only strangers.

My life continued along these lines for nearly forty years, and as my inner rage grew, so did the incidences of people going out of their way to cause me grief. I was thirty-nine, working in a wood shop building custom furniture, and I was very good at it. One weekend day while driving down a street in Kansas City, I noticed a man carrying an antique Queen Anne chair to a Dumpster in an apartment complex. I could see that the chair had a broken rung, a problem I could easily fix. That chair was worth money—something I desperately needed—so I quickly turned into the complex and stopped my car beside the Dumpster. As the man approached I asked, "If you're going to throw that away, may I have it?"

"*No*," he replied as he smashed it over the side of the Dumpster. I watched in disbelief as the old wood shattered on impact. Too stunned to even reply, I drove off.

What a complete and total lowlife, I thought to myself, *he didn't want it, but he would rather destroy it than give it to someone who could fix it and use it.* Once again, I had more evidence that God was out to get me by working through other people.

Finally, about a year later, I had suffered all I could stand. There was no fight left in me; I couldn't go on. I was tired, tired of struggling to get up only to be knocked back down again, tired of failing, tired of fighting against the world, tired of living.

Although I still had a strong fear of death, that fear was overpowered by my fear of life. That was my situation on the cold winter day that was supposed to be the last day of my life. I drove my car down along the Missouri River just outside Kansas City, parked and walked downstream. My plan was simple; I wore a heavy winter coat that would aid the frigid, rushing water in pulling me under. Knowing that I was a coward, and that once I hit the water I would probably chicken out, I walked far from my car so I would stand a better chance of freezing to death before I could make it back. I was serious, deadly serious. I found a place where I could easily climb down to the water's edge; I stood for a moment looking at the ice chunks floating past. There was no hesitation, merely a moment to take one last look around before letting myself fall into the river. My life was nearly over, and I felt a sense of relief.

Then suddenly, unbidden, the memory of that man with the chair at the Dumpster flooded through my mind. I was looking at the rushing river which was about to relieve me of the burden of life, yet what I was seeing was the chair smashing into a thousand splinters. Then a voice came from my own imagination, or from right beside me; I can not swear which. It said, "If you're going to throw that away, may I have it?" and I knew that it was the voice of God. In a millisecond my mind flooded with thoughts of the man I had been all my life, the people I had hurt, the destruction that lay behind me. Yet at that moment, I knew beyond all doubt that God loved me, not because of what I had done, but in spite of what I had done. Not because of who I am, but because of who God is . . . *unconditional love*.

I fell to my knees and cried tears of shame, pain and joy. At that moment I knew that I wanted to give my life to God. At the time I had no idea how I would do it, but I knew that if God could fix me and use me, I would not be like the man with the chair at the Dumpster.

On that cold wintry day on the bank of the Missouri River, circumstances caused me to become willing. As it turned out, all I had to do to give my life to God was become *willing. Willing* to listen to inner guidance, *willing* to do whatever God puts in front of me, *willing* to trust that God will not give me a task beyond my abilities, *willing* to accept that God is more concerned about my welfare than I am, *willing* to recognize that everything I thought I knew could be wrong, *willing* to see the truth . . . even when it hurts. *Willing* to try to let go of my hate, so my hands are free to grasp love. And even when I fall short on all other counts, I need to be *willing* to become *willing,* and to understand, from the depths of my being, that there is nothing I can do to keep the love of God from man.

Victor Fried

Goin' Fishin'

For years, Uncle Mike and I fished the little lake near home every chance we got. As we grew older, though, our families and work became more and more important while the fishing trips got fewer and farther between. One unforgettable weekend, Uncle Mike and I did manage to find time for a fishing tournament—by default, mind you—our wives were on a church retreat and we men were home alone.

The first day of the event was a Saturday. Fishing conditions couldn't have been better—cool water, a light breeze and just a touch of cloud cover. We spent the whole time catching and releasing fish too small to keep—a typical day of fishing for both of us. When we decided to pack it in, the final tally was just three fish—seven pounds total. On the second day, the weather wasn't quite as friendly. The wind blew so bad we allowed ourselves to drift into a large cove for shelter. There, we strung a long line between two trees so we could steady our boat before the start of a relaxing day of drowning worms.

It wasn't long before we noticed a young boy in an aluminum johnboat at the very back of the cove, almost to the lone dock. He had paddled out a little way and was tied up to a big tree at the edge of the water. As we drifted in his direction—without a bite for what seemed like forever—we noticed the lad catching a fish every few minutes. You know how it is; when you're frustrated, you want to know what bait a "lucky" fisherman is using. As we got closer, Uncle Mike and I watched as the boy baited a hook and dropped his line straight down by the big tree. Just like before, only four or five minutes later, he caught what appeared to be another bass in the several-pounds range. Unable to resist our curiosity, Uncle Mike and I had to talk to the young angler.

"Whatcha usin' for bait?" I inquired.

"Stinging worms, sir."

"What was that?" I asked, not sure I'd heard him right.

"Stinging worms," he repeated.

Uncle Mike and I looked at each other. Neither of us had any idea what a "stinging worm" was. As we watched the boy bait his hook again, we noticed him jump and yank his hand away from the bait can. Then he reached in again and pulled out a large brown worm. This called for a closer look, and we eased up alongside the johnboat.

"Can we see those worms? We might need to go buy us some," I said with a grin.

"Sure, here. But you can't buy 'em. I got these under a log behind my house."

Uncle Mike reached over and took the can. We both looked inside at the same time. In a fraction of a second, we knew—snakes. These were small rattlesnakes; and about ten of them were left! Uncle Mike asked if he could see the boy's hands. We soon saw that they were covered with small welts—snakebites.

Uncle Mike said, "Son, these aren't stinging worms. These are baby rattlesnakes, and you need to go to the hospital—*now!*" The poor little angler's face went pale.

"My mom and dad are at home. I gotta go see 'em," the frightened boy blurted. We immediately untied his boat and towed him over to the dock. As we helped him out, we noticed he had turned white as a sheet. He said his right arm and stomach were starting to hurt. I picked the boy up and carried him to his parents' house. His mom was in the kitchen preparing lunch. We immediately called 911 and kept the boy quiet until the ambulance came. I rode to the hospital with him and his mom, carrying the can of "stinging worms" to show the emergency room doctor. The little guy was very lucky. Although he got quite sick and the pain was real bad early on, he recovered completely.

No surprise—Uncle Mike and I didn't place in that tournament. Usually when I skip church to go fishing, I reckon God isn't going to let me catch anything anyway. However, on that particular Sunday, he had other plans for us.

T. J. Greaney

Angels Among Us

January 25, 1986—I'll never forget that night! My band and I were driving back to Nashville after performing at a police benefit in Albertville, Alabama. It was raining hard, and our van and trailer were stopped at a light as we waited to cross a four-lane highway. I was sitting in the back of the van on the left, and our road manager, Randy, was driving. As I looked out the window, I saw an eighteen-wheeler barreling down the highway toward the intersection. I thought to myself, *My God, if his light turns red, that truck driver's not going to be able to stop his rig!*

As I looked up, I saw our light turn green. . . . all in what must have been a split second. But it seemed like forever, and ever, and ever. . . . as if everything had suddenly switched to slow motion. I felt Randy lift his foot off the brake—we started moving forward—and I got an awful sick feeling deep in the pit of my stomach.

"Stop!" I yelled at Randy, sensing that he didn't see the truck. Randy jammed on the brakes just as the eighteen-wheeler—air horn blasting—slammed into us. Miraculously, the truck just clipped the front-left side of my Dodge maxivan—the strongest part. Our equipment-packed trailer was ripped off its hitch as our van spun

around on the wet pavement. Although the Dodge was totaled, we all survived with minimal injuries. Had the collision occurred just a moment later, we would have been broadsided and—from what the police officers told us—most likely killed.

So it had come to pass. . . . The angelic prophecy was manifested. . . .

Shortly before Christmas 1985, I had started getting premonitions that I was going to be in a bad vehicle accident. Night after night, I lay in bed, drifting off to sleep when suddenly I'd sit up with my heart pounding, thinking to myself, *I'm not ready to go yet!* Each time, I was overwhelmed by a sense of despair—a sick feeling deep in the pit of my stomach. This went on for weeks, right on through the holidays. I feared I might lose my mind! Then, in the wee hours of the morning of January 24, 1986, something very weird happened.

I was in my kitchen, making a birthday cake—chocolate, of course—for a gathering I was having the next afternoon to celebrate my birthday. As I stirred the batter, "something" took hold of me and urged me to go outside. I wasn't really scared, but I felt very uneasy—like when you're getting ready to hear something you don't want to hear. I stood in the front yard, looked up at the starry sky and asked out loud, "What? What is it you're trying to tell me?"

I didn't have to wait long for an answer. This loud, very strong, masculine voice said, *"Be careful—this may be your last birthday!"* I felt slammed by that same sick feeling in my stomach that I got when I was having those bedtime premonitions. I just stood there in the yard, dumbfounded, asking out loud for more information, but no more was given. I knew I was being warned about something, and I had a pretty good idea that it was connected to my premonitions.

I went back in the house. My knees were shaking and my heart was pounding. My mind kept going over every word. . . . "Be—careful—this—may—be—your—last—birthday!"

"May" is the key word, I thought to myself. Whatever I was being warned about must be something I can prevent—otherwise, why am I being warned? And who was it that was warning me? At the time, I thought it was God, or my sweet, loving daddy (who passed away in 1982) speaking to me in a voice not quite his own. . . . much deeper than I remembered.

After the accident, I realized that the voice from above belonged to my guardian angel. As soon as I understood that, I wrote down the title, "Angels Among Us," in my notebook and started thinking about lyrics off and on for several years. It wasn't until Christmas 1992, when I was sitting in my dad's old easy chair late one night at my mom's house, that I got the strongest feeling I had to finish the song. When I got back to Nashville, I worked with Don Goodman—a good friend and a great songwriter—and we put the finishing touches to "Angels Among Us."

Not long afterward, the song was recorded by Alabama. Since then, I've had a hard time keeping track of the number of phone calls, faxes and letters I've received about how "Angels Among Us" has touched people's lives. One of the best things happened right before Christmas 1996.

My husband, Duane, and I were in California, where he was playing a gig with Glenn Frey. That's when I got an urgent call from Kim Armstrong in Alabama's Ft. Payne office. Kim, voice cracking, told me that a nine-year-old girl in Virginia had been in a coma for twelve days following a bad car crash. The child had head injuries so extensive her doctor saw little chance of recovery. He suggested that the mother try playing some music for the little girl. When the chorus of "Angels Among Us" began, the little girl woke up and started crying—just as she and her mother had done before the little girl's accident when they listened to the song together.

In the next few days, the article about the little girl appeared in newspapers all over the country, and my phone rang off the hook. A few weeks later, I got to talk with the little girl's mother. She said it looked like her daughter would have a complete recovery, and the child was already back at school!

That one bit of news made my whole Christmas! Maybe writing this song was one of the reasons I wasn't taken on January 25, 1986. I hope there are more reasons. Lots more!

Becky Hobbs

Nuns in the Country

Two nuns were driving down a country road when they ran out of gas. They walked to a farmhouse and a farmer gave them some gasoline; but the only container he had was an old bedpan. The nuns were happy to take whatever they were offered and returned to their car.

As they were pouring the gasoline from the bedpan into the tank of their car, a minister drove by. He stopped, rolled down his window and said, "Excuse me, sisters. I'm not of your religion, but I couldn't help admiring your faith!"

Dan Clark

When the Frog Got His Wings

With all the innocence of a six-year-old, I asked, "Bob, are you prejudiced?"

Never looking up, he replied, "Everybody's prejudiced—black, white, men, women—everybody."

Not to be disregarded that easily, I continued, "Well, what are you prejudiced against?"

"Sin," he said as he shined his customer's shoes to a mirror finish.

Somehow, I sensed that our conversation was finished. *Bob must be weary,* I thought. And when Bob was weary, he didn't want to talk—not to me, not to anyone.

No matter. My attention had already been diverted to the popping sounds of the razor strop as the barber sharpened his blade to a fine edge. The broad smile on the barber's face clearly said, *Bob got the best of you again, didn't he?*

I ignored the stupid barber and returned my attention to Bob. Looking up at his customer, who had just handed him a half-dollar and turned to walk away, Bob said, "Too much, sir. The tip's got to relate to the price." Back then, the price for a shoe shine was fifteen cents. Bob handed the bewildered customer a quarter and thanked him for his business.

My conversations with Bob Watkins continued with some regularity over the next several years. During that time, Bob became my friend, my confidant and my teacher—quite a different relationship from the one evident from our first meeting.

My first trip to the barbershop—sometime near my fourth birthday—was a total disaster. The fear associated with my first haircut was more than enough to unnerve me. Then I saw Bob. I burst into tears and was about to run from the barbershop, when a soft, deep voice summoned me to the shoe shine chair. I looked slightly upward into the most radiant face I had ever seen. The sparkling eyes and toothy grin, beaming from the coal black face erased all my fears.

Instinctively, I was drawn to Bob despite his appearance. His ebony face, with the large indentation in his forehead, always glistened. His short legs didn't match his upper body, giving the appearance of a man on the legs of a child. But his feet—those huge feet encased in giant black shoes—turned backward, and this was more than I could comprehend. And, when he sat back in a resting position on the tops of the shoes, Bob looked forever like a giant frog, ready to leap at any moment.

I later learned that both of Bob's feet had been amputated, just above the ankle, in a railroad accident—the same accident that left the ugly indentation in his forehead. It then became clear. Bob's feet were not backward; he had no feet. He stood, and even walked, on his knees and lower legs which were covered with the large, cushioned black leather shoes, giving the appearance of abnormally large feet turned backward.

From time to time, I tried walking on my knees and lower legs, but after a few minutes, the pain was unbearable. I then realized that Bob must have been in severe pain, each day of his life. Some time later, it occurred to me to wonder why Bob spent his days quoting Scripture and praising God, the same God who allowed the accident, the pain and the suffering. I was even more perplexed.

Evidently Bob sensed my confusion, for one day when the barbershop was empty, Bob motioned me to sit in the shoe shine chair. There, he described in detail the railroad accident and his hospital recovery. Bob said he had been a bitter young man, unhappy with life and seemingly unable to change his destiny. He claimed that he had been a drunkard, a gambler, a womanizer and a whore-monger. I didn't know what a womanizer or a whore-monger was, but I guessed that they must have been pretty bad, being listed with drunkard and gambler, terms familiar to me even at my early age.

Bob explained that he had spent the night with another man's wife, leaving during the early morning hours before her husband returned. Drunk, without money and totally disgusted with himself, he attempted to board a freight train for the short ride to the railroad station. He lost his footing on the side ladder of the railroad car and fell to the tracks. A few minutes of excruciating pain were followed by total darkness.

A week or so later, Bob regained consciousness in a hospital bed—without feet. Bandages covered the ugly indentation in his forehead as well as the cuts and severe abrasions on the trunk of his body. He was at the point of death, with no will to live, cursing God and everyone around him.

After a while, as he regained his strength, he noticed a Bible on the bedside table. For some inexplicable reason, Bob started spending his time looking at the Good Book. Then, one day he noticed that the Bible was open. His curiosity aroused, Bob picked up the Bible and began reading about a man called Job. He was intrigued by Job— and later by other men of the Bible who had endured great hardships, yet remained faithful to God. Bob could relate to these men—at least to their hardships.

His reading was slow, lingering a moment on each word. Later, he bought a dictionary, and much later, biblical reference books. But for his long hospital stay, Bob was content with reading slowly. Sometimes he read all day and well into the night. In his condition, at this point in his life, time meant nothing. He had nowhere to run.

Ultimately, Bob Watkins's life was transformed from drunkard, gambler, womanizer and whoremonger to servant of God. And with this transformation came a radiance—a glow—that masked the ugliness of his injuries. Together with an uncanny understanding of both the Bible and life itself, he blamed his accident and injuries not on God, but on his sinful ways. He claimed, without reservation, that the accident was his blessing. From that accident, Bob had found God, and with God at his side, he had a life with fullness and meaning.

At the close of each business day, Bob struggled to slide his heavy shoes, one in front of the other, down the main street of town on his long journey home—a furnished room in an old, deteriorating building a half mile from the barbershop. He stopped every so often to look toward the surrounding mountains, particularly Keeny's Knob, the highest and most majestic of all the mountains surrounding this quiet, rural valley town. According to Bob, "God is everywhere, but he likes the mountains best—that's where he gave Moses the Ten Commandments and allowed him to see the Promised Land; that's where Noah's ark landed. Most of the great events of the Bible happened on a mountain or at the foot of a mountain."

Bob rarely walked or shuffled more than a block from the barbershop, though. Passing motorists, often by design, almost always stopped to give Bob a ride home or to work and, on Sundays, to church. It didn't make much difference to Bob which church he attended, as long as God was inside and God's people filled the pews. To no one's surprise, Bob was welcome in every church in town—black and white.

Nevertheless, Bob was somewhat partial to one of the white churches. The pastor of that church often huddled with Bob on a regular basis in a corner of the barbershop deep in private conversation. The barber invariably laughed and whispered to his customers, "The preacher's getting his sermon for next Sunday."

Of all the people I have known in this life, Bob Watkins was the only person totally without prejudice. He was also loved and respected by everyone he met, regardless of race, color or religion. Even the worst of sinners were welcomed by Bob with love and kindness. Bob reasoned that he was commissioned to do that which Jesus would have done, including offering love and kindness toward the most despicable of humankind.

To me, Bob Watkins was without fault, except maybe for the times he claimed he was "weary" and didn't want to talk. On those occasions, he seemed almost to be in a trance, transfixed on someone, or something, or some-place far away. My father said that Bob knew so much about heaven he was forever homesick.

Sometime before midnight on a clear summer night, our Heavenly Father called Bob Watkins home. Bob was found the next morning by his landlady—slumped in his dilapidated easy chair—with a smile on his face. His tattered old Bible was opened to the book of Acts. A part of Acts 7:55 was underlined, which read, ". . . looked up to Heaven and saw the glory of God, and Jesus standing at the right hand of God." On the floor, beside the easy chair, lay a small white feather.

The frog finally got his wings.

H. R. Ayers

$$\overline{4}$$

LIVING
THE DREAM

When you stop dreaming, you stop living.

Lorrie Morgan

What It Takes

One of my most memorable experiences took place when I worked as Associate Director of ASCAP in Nashville. At the time, Rod Phelps, one of my Texas friends, asked me to talk with a new guy he was sending to see me. You must understand that in the music business, it's common courtesy to listen to your friends and spend time with the people they send you. Soon after talking with Rod, the new guy dropped by my office and played me some songs. I remember I didn't pull any punches; I told him his songs were only "fair."

In the middle of our conversation, I was distracted when one of my writers—a guy with money problems—barged in. I asked my guest to excuse me a moment while I got the writer some paperwork to support a bank loan application. Later, I asked the new guy to keep the writer's situation confidential because it was a private matter. My guest responded, "Man, I recognize that writer. *He* needs a bank loan?"

"Yeah! *Everybody* needs help now and then," I told him.

Overhearing the conversation the guy caught the amount of money that the writer needed. My guest said he made more than that in a week playing in Oklahoma.

"If that's the case, you'd better get on back to Oklahoma. You'll never make that kind of money playing the clubs in Nashville. I've got this saying: 'We create music in Nashville, and we sell it in Texas.' You can certainly include Oklahoma in there, too," I added.

The new guy laughed, "Well I just can't believe that. What if I bring my whole band down here?"

"How many is in your band?" I asked.

"Five."

"Well," I said, "you and five other guys will starve to death in Nashville," I predicted.

Sensing that I'd offended my guest, I tried to make amends by telling him, "Those are just the facts in this town. If you want to come here and write, if you want to make it as an artist, it's going to be tough. However, I'll be glad to help you. I'll see you at 9:00 tomorrow morning right here in my office. Since my friend, Rod, sent you to me, I'm going to do what I can to help you." Later, I learned that my guest had the use of Rod's personal credit cards so the guy could get to Nashville—that's how much Rod believed in his potential. "You be here at 9:00, and I'll help you find a place to live," I promised.

Well, at 9:00 the next morning, the Oklahoma guy didn't show. I waited 'til about 10:30 before I called Rod and asked if he'd seen him. "No, I thought he was with you," was the response.

I told Rod the guy was *supposed* to be with me. That bothered Rod because, well, this guy always kept his appointments. That afternoon, Rod called to let me know what had happened. His guy was all upset with me and was headed back to Oklahoma. I explained that all I did was just tell him the truth. "Man, if he can't take the truth, well, I'm sorry. I just told him the way things are in a detailed story of what has to be done to make it in Nashville."

That was the end of it—or so I thought. About a year later, this Oklahoma guy came back. But instead of seeing me, he walked right past my office and down the hall to talk with my associate. Soon after, the two of them struck a deal. I guess the guy didn't particularly want to see me. A few months later, this associate left ASCAP and opened a publishing company with the guy from Oklahoma.

Several months later, I attended a "Writer's Night" at Nashville's Blue Bird Café. To my surprise, the Oklahoma guy was filling in for a writer who didn't show up. A few months later, he was signed to Capitol Records and recorded his first album. At that time, the president of Capitol Records was a friend of mine named Joe Smith. I sent Joe the guy's advance tape and told him to give special attention to this young man. I told Joe this guy was a friend of mine, and he's going to be a "monster" artist. Joe took my advice. Capitol Records spent a lot of money on the new artist and did everything necessary to help him become a huge success.

After this guy hit the top, he told everybody who would listen that everything I'd said had been true. Since then, he has thanked me many times. Not long ago, the now-legendary country star and I got together. He said, "Merle, you remember that first meeting we had in Nashville? Has it already been ten years? I'll *never* forget it!"

This story just goes to show that it takes more than being friends—it takes talent, persistence, focus and hard work—to survive and become a superstar in the entertainment business.

Just ask my friend, Garth Brooks.

Merlin Littlefield

In the Footsteps of a Good Man

If you're dedicated, if it's something that lives and breathes in your heart, then you've simply got to go ahead and do it.

Rodney Crowell

I always knew I was the different one in my family. They all seemed normal. Whereas, from the day I picked up a guitar, I was obsessed. Before I was ten years old, I began to eat, sleep and dream bluegrass and country music. I had every album and I could play along. My hero of heroes was Lester Flatt. By the time I was eleven, I knew I wanted to be just like him.

When I was twelve years old, in 1971, I got a friend to take me to Bill Monroe's festival in Bean Blossom, Indiana. The whole thing was magic, but nothing mattered as much as the fact that Lester Flatt would be playing in person. I had the concert schedule memorized, and before it was time for Lester Flatt to play, I found his bus. It was a vision in diesel. It looked like a rolling billboard, painted with "Lester Flatt and the Nashville Grass Sponsored by Martha White Flour."

When Lester Flatt came out, the speech I'd planned for about seven years got lost inside of me. It was all I could do to ask for an autograph. As I followed him on the long walk to the stage, I noticed the way he cocked his hat on his head—and the effect he had on the campers. As he walked through, they sort of stood straighter. It was like the effect of a preacher walking through a poker game.

I followed in his wake, knowing I was walking in the footsteps of a good man.

I left the festival even more on fire with the thrill of music. That summer I spent as much time as I could around local musician Carl Jackson. Carl's daddy was a musician, too, and he spent lots of hours working with me on the mandolin. Carl had gone on the road with several musicians, and the next year, he joined the Sullivan Family, a popular bluegrass gospel group. When the Sullivan Family was slated to play at a church near my home, I persuaded Enoch Sullivan, the patriarch, to let me play on a couple of songs. Oh, it was wonderful!

I was totally hooked. I begged and pleaded with Carl until he asked Enoch if I could go on the road with them that summer, and Enoch agreed. I felt my life had begun.

We played mostly Pentecostal churches on the back roads of the Deep South. People loved the Sullivan Family and welcomed us everywhere we went. When we played a festival at Lavonia, Georgia, I ran into Roland White. Roland played with Lester Flatt, and I'd met him the year before at Bean Blossom. We hung out some—at a bluegrass festival, hanging out means sitting around playing music.

Can you imagine the ecstasy of a twelve-year-old boy jamming with Roland White? What could make it more perfect?

I'll tell you what—when the festival was over, Roland gave me his phone number and said if I could get permission from my parents to go on the road with them one weekend, to give him a call.

After a summer with the Sullivan Family, I knew that "the road" is a powerful thing. It has a way of changing and claiming you. Some people just aren't cut out for it, but I loved it from the beginning. Mostly, to me, the road meant freedom. That's what I had to give up when it was time to go back to school.

Not surprisingly, after spending the summer in my dream world I was a poor excuse for a student. The final straw came one day when a teacher came up behind me when I was supposed to be reading history and I had a *Country Music Roundup* inside my history book. She busted me.

"Marty," she said, "You could make something out of yourself if you'd get your mind off music and get it on history."

"Ma'am," I replied, "I'm more into *making* history than learning about it."

On the strength of that remark—and something about my attitude and haircut—I was excused from school.

My poor parents. I'm sure they expected me to be sad and sorry about my situation. Instead, of course, I was formulating a plan. I suddenly had a few unexpected days free.

As soon as I got home, I called Roland to see if his invitation was still open. He got an okay from Lester. Before my parents even had a chance to discuss "my situation" with me, I met them crying, begging and pleading to join Roland White for the weekend. My parents knew full well who Lester Flatt was. They also knew that this was an extraordinary opportunity. So instead of spending the weekend grounded, as I'm sure my teacher intended, I was on a bus to Nashville!

The old bus station in Nashville was across the street from the Ryman Auditorium. When I got off the bus, I paused, purposely thinking of where I'd come from. Then I took a look at the Opry to see where I wanted to go.

Within a couple of hours, I was on that bus I'd dreamed about, heading off with the guys toward Delaware for the weekend. As we traveled, Roland and I got out the mandolin and guitar and started playing some tunes. Lester came back to go to bed and stopped for a minute to listen. I guess he liked what he heard, 'cause he laughed and said, "Why don't you do a couple of songs on the show tomorrow?"

That pretty much made my year.

Lester let me play all four shows the band did over the next two days. He was generous and gracious, building me up and giving me recognition during the shows.

When the weekend was over, I figured my life was downhill from there. How on earth would I ever pay attention to history when I'd played with Lester Flatt? I'd reached my dream; I'd grabbed the brass ring. Everything else would certainly seem drab and gray in comparison.

On Sunday, when the band was packing, I thanked Lester for letting me play with them. As I did, I could see the wheels turning in his head: old act, new blood, this might work. Also, in the space of a couple of days we had a routine of gags between us. The chemistry was there, and we had the beginnings of a friendship.

Lester suggested that if we could work out something about school, he would talk to my parents about joining him full-time.

I used most of the pay phones between Delaware and Tennessee begging my parents for a little more time. I had a lot to tell them—Lester had invited me to play the Friday night Opry, Roland had a hat I could use, I had money left over, and, oh, yes—Lester had offered me a job.

"A job? Marty, you're in junior high school! You're thirteen years old!"

"Don't say yes or no now, Dad, please! One week—just give me one more week. Let me play the Opry."

Tuesday at WSM radio was just business for Lester and the guys after so many years. But just last week, I'd been listening to this show at home, dreaming, just dreaming. And now . . .

Announcer Grant Turner read his Martha White script and added, "along with special guests Mac Wiseman and Marty Stuart."

Dear God, I hoped my history teacher listened to that show!

I remember thinking and praying a lot that week. I was definitely happy, kind of lonesome and kind of amazed at how fast everything had happened. I not only prayed for guidance for myself, I prayed for my mom and dad—especially Mom. I asked God to comfort her and let her know I was all right.

And I thought realistically about my future. There was no family business to go into. I didn't think I had a future as a cotton farmer, and I couldn't see myself at a factory; two occupations chosen by many kids in my school.

So what *did* I want out of life?

I wanted to go places, see things, meet all sorts of people. Most of all, I wanted to live in the world of country music. That Friday night, one week after I'd gotten off the bus and set my sights on the Opry, I was playing there. Roy Acuff, Tex Ritter, Brother Oswald . . . the number of greats performing that night went on and on. And then there was . . . Marty Stuart.

Yes, this was my world. This was where I wanted to be.

But was the timing wrong? Would I lose it all because I'd made it across the street in one week instead of in ten years?

I know that letting your thirteen-year-old go out into the world must have been a heavy decision. And, to tell you the truth, I don't think my folks would have let me do it with anyone but Lester.

Lester arranged to meet with my folks in person. He assured them that I'd be well looked after, that I'd keep a little spending money and send the rest of my earnings to the bank. He was already talking to Lance Leroy, our manager, (*our* manager!) about the details of how to finish my education.

To this day, I'm sure that the thing that made the difference was that Lester Flatt promised to personally assume responsibility for me. Even in that short of a time, my parents could see that Lester was a man of integrity, a man of his word.

My parents agreed to give it a try. I told my mom and dad and sister good-bye and climbed onto the bus. As their cars faded from sight in the Alabama dust, I had to fight back tears. But I knew that beyond that cloud of dust there was a big world waiting, and I wanted to see it—every bit.

Marty Stuart

A Little More Out of Life

Always be "work in progress."

Tim DuBois

I wanted the job more than anything in my life. I was a veteran, a grown man, ready to marry and settle down, but I couldn't keep a job and I was discouraged, all because I stuttered.

I had worked as a strawberry picker, a house painter, and even a fireman for the Atlantic Coast Line Railroad. I lost that job because by the time I was able to call out the train signals ahead we were already four or five miles down the track.

Then I heard that a candy company in Plant City, Florida, was looking for a route driver. And I'd heard that the owner of the company, a man named Miller, was a former stutterer who had somehow learned to control his stutter. A fellow sufferer, I was sure, would certainly understand and hire me. I set my heart on getting that job.

I got an appointment with Mr. Miller. When his secretary ushered me into his office, Mr. Miller, a kindly looking man who wore wire-rimmed glasses, looked me over.

Then he asked why I wanted the job.

I couldn't think of anything smart to say; I just started blurting the simple truth. "B-b-because I need the m-m-money," I sputtered. I knew I sounded terrible, but I thought, *Well, at least he's hearing me at my worst.*

For a long time, Mr. Miller didn't say anything. Then finally he looked me straight in the eye. "Mr. Tillis," he said softly, "I'm not going to give you a job."

I stared at him, dumbfounded. He must have seen the surprise in my face.

"Oh, don't get me wrong," he said. "I think you'd do well. It's just that I don't have an opening right now." Then he reached into his desk drawer and pulled out a piece of paper, worn and tattered. "I'd like you to take this home and read it," he said. "Read it every night for a month."

Hardly hearing his words, I reached out numbly, took the paper and stuck it in my pocket. Tears of disappointment burned my eyes. I turned my head away, told him good-bye and slumped out of the Miller Candy Company.

That night I felt totally dejected. *Who wants a stutterer around?* I asked myself in defeat. Nobody. And as long as I stuttered I would be a nobody. I had lived with this pain all my life.

I didn't know that I talked differently until I started school. When I tried to talk everybody laughed. I began to withdraw more and more into myself.

My mother often said that God would help me solve my problem. I couldn't see how. We were Baptists, but once a week Mama would take me up the road to a little Pentecostal church. I loved to listen to the singing in there, the guitars and the fiddles they used in those mid-week services. And when I joined in the singing, I noticed that I didn't stutter at all.

Mama would hold family songfests on the front porch every evening, all of us sitting around and singing for hours; I didn't stutter a word. We found out that when a stutterer speaks, air gets trapped in his throat. But when he sings, for some reason the breathing apparatus works normally and there is no stutter. I sometimes wondered if I might go through life singing, never having to talk again.

But after the interview with Mr. Miller, I was prepared never to utter another sound. I took the piece of paper he had given me out of my pocket, ready to tear it to shreds. But something made me look at it. It was a prayer—a very well-known one, but one I didn't know at the time: "God, grant me the serenity to accept the things I cannot change, the courage to change the things I can, and the wisdom to know the difference."

I read the words again. Then again. They were like the light at the end of a tunnel.

Accept the things I cannot change. I could work at easing my stuttering, I knew, but I probably could never really change the way I talked.

Courage to change the things I can. What I could do something about were all my fears—fear of stepping out of my shell, fear of trying to be somebody, fear of thinking bigger than I had been doing.

God, grant me the serenity. Here, I knew, was the key to the whole prayer. When, I wondered, was the last time I actually had reached out to God? Years earlier, when I was a kid, I had prayed that I would wake up one morning and talk differently. When it didn't happen, I forgot about God. But from what I was feeling now, I was pretty sure that the Lord hadn't forgotten about me.

Soon I was asleep—a deep and restful sleep. But though serenity came that night, it didn't hang around all the time. And change didn't come overnight either. I kept reciting that prayer, reminding myself of its words and their meaning, till I finally could place myself in God's hands, in trust, without fear of what might happen to me.

I gradually grew aware of a desire deep within me to write songs, the kind of country music songs we had sung in the Pentecostal church. I learned to play the guitar and started writing. At the same time, I often thought of how enjoyable it would be to stand up in front of people and entertain them, but I knew this was a daydream because of my stutter.

Some months later, armed with some of my songs, I went to Nashville in hopes of getting somebody to listen to my work. One door led to another, and one day I got an appointment to audition for Minnie Pearl, one of the biggest names and greatest people in country music.

I was scared. As I went to the studio, I kept praying: "Your serenity, Lord. Your serenity."

The audition went well and Minnie Pearl hired me as a backup musician and a songwriter. I was happy, but I stayed in the background for years and years, nowhere near my daydream of standing up and doing the entertaining myself, still frightened of what people would think of my Porky Pig stammer.

Then, in 1970, Glen Campbell invited me to be an accompanying musician on his *Goodtime Hour* television show. We used to kid around with one another, and one day backstage I found myself trading jokes with Glen and some of his guests.

"Hey, Mel," Glen said, suddenly serious, "you're funny, you know that?"

"Yeah," I said, laughing, "really funny."

But Glen wanted me to know he wasn't kidding. "I'd like to use you on the show, have you introduce yourself in a skit."

"No way!" I said.

I kept trying to back out, but Glen and a few others wouldn't hear of it. They helped me to rehearse what I'd say to the audience, but I was so nervous that the few lines I practiced kept coming out as messed up as a two-headed calf.

The night before we were to tape the show, I called my wife, Doris, at our home in Tennessee. "I don't know what I got myself into, honey," I said, "but right now I feel like I want out."

Before I knew it, a bunch of yelling broke out on the telephone, not just from Doris but from our four kids who were on other extensions. "Daddy, you better do it," said my boy Mel Jr. "I told all my friends you were going to talk on television."

I gulped. Then Doris, in her soothing way, said, "I hope you realize we're all behind you. Don't be afraid."

Afraid. Yep, that's what I was. When I hung up the phone, my mind went back to a scrap of paper. Its words by now were as clear in my memory as they must have been on that paper when Mr. Miller first wrote them. *God* . . . I began silently.

The next day, I went to face the TV cameras. "The other d-d-day, somebody asked me when I was going to b-b-be on television." I stuttered to the audience, trying to get out my introduction to my song. "I t-t-told them two years. I just w-w-wasn't sure when I w-w-would ever finish th-th-this introduction."

To my amazement, everybody laughed along with me. And my fear got drowned out in the laughter. I could poke fun at myself, and people would respond—not in ridicule, but in warmth and fun. The audience would accept me, just as I was. And, more important, the prayer that Mr. Miller gave me had finally taught me to accept myself.

Mel Tillis

Just a Plain Ol' Country Girl

Keep learning, keep doing and get your ducks in a row. Then, when opportunity knocks, you're ready.

Buck Owens

I was twenty-eight years old, the age when most young people have their eyes firmly fixed on the promise of success—and I was a failure. Life had reached a dead end for Sarah Ophelia Cannon, the aspiring dramatic actress from Centerville, Tennessee.

Six years earlier, fresh from Ward-Belmont College, I had joined a theatrical production company in Atlanta, and had been going into small towns and rural communities producing country-style musical comedies. But now, in the summer of 1940, the country was in a depression, radio and changing times had altered people's tastes, and amateur shows weren't all that big anymore.

So, jobless and with nothing else in sight, I went back to Centerville. To bring some money into the house, I finally got a WPA job as a recreation-room director. It paid fifty dollars a month, for which I was grateful, but it sure was a dull job.

I felt so frustrated in my plan to be a dramatic star that I kept praying, "God, where, where, where do I go? What do I do?" And when no answers came to me, I found myself questioning God in despair.

Restless and dissatisfied though I was, it was nice in a way, to be back home. I tried to relieve the dullness of my job by teaching some of the town's youngsters music and drama. And when I got a chance, I'd try my luck as a performer, myself. I'd dress up as this rangy country girl, which I was anyway, and tell little stories and jokes that I'd picked up during my years with the production company, living around country folk. I gave this country girl a name—Minnie Pearl.

Summer faded, and my spirits sank lower and lower. One dreary October afternoon I was in the WPA recreation room, waiting for the children to thunder down on me when a banker friend, Jim Walker, came in.

"Ophelia," he said, "we're going to have a banker's convention here. I understand that in the evenings you've been teaching some children dramatics and dancing and singing. Would you let the children entertain the bankers?"

I said, yes, of course. He started to walk away, then he stopped and turned. "Oh, by the way," he added, "the speaker from Chicago is flying into Nashville and then driving to Centerville. If he's late, would you mind doing that thing you do?"

"You mean Minnie Pearl?"

"That's it. Would you kill time with this Minnie Pearl thing until the speaker gets here?"

I told Jim I'd do it.

That night we performed for the bankers. The children sang and danced to old-time, popular songs while I was backstage, disheveled and frantic, getting the children off and on the stage.

We finished the program, and Jim came backstage. "The speaker's not here yet, Ophelia. You'll have to help us."

"All right," I told him. "Just give me a minute to straighten up." Then I went out in front of the hundred or so men in the audience and said, "I'd like to give you my interpretation of the mountain girl, Minnie Pearl."

I started telling them about the marvelous, mythical town of Grinder's Switch, about my Uncle Nabob and Aunt Ambrosia and Brother and his dog and the horseshoe and all those silly things. And the bankers were laughing and applauding. When I ran out of stories, I looked over at Jim, and he shook his head.

"No," he said, "he's not here yet!"

So I went over to the piano and started playing and singing—"Maple on the Hill" and "Careless Love" and "Red River Valley" and a lot of other old country songs. The men loved it.

After I'd sung awhile, and still no speaker, I said to the audience, "Well, let's just all sing." The men joined me in "My Wild Irish Rose" and "Let Me Call You Sweetheart."

Then finally Jim came over to me and said, "He's here. You can stop now."

The men shouted, "Oh, no! Let's sing some more!" I smiled real big, thanked them real big and turned the program back over to Jim.

When I got home, Mama asked me how it went. "Oh, pretty well," I said. I had just spent the evening clowning. It didn't mean anything.

But one of the bankers in the audience, Bob Turner, knew Harry Stone, the manager of the great country music station in Nashville, WSM. "Harry," he told him, "there's a girl down in Centerville who belongs on that Grand Ole Opry. She's down on her luck. I know her family; I come from down that way—and if you can give her a break, it sure would be a big favor to me."

Harry Stone said all right and had me come up for an audition. And that changed my whole life. It was the beginning of Minnie Pearl, and, to me, the beginning of a new way to look at things.

I saw at last that I had become a failure only because I wouldn't accept what I truly was. I had been trying to become something I couldn't be. I would never be a great dramatic actress; I was Minnie Pearl, a plain, comic country girl, poking fun at herself and sharing that fun with others. When I learned to accept that role, the one God had given me, he turned my failure into success.

Sarah Ophelia Cannon

Confidence Builder

True country music is honesty, sincerity and real life to the hilt.

Garth Brooks

Times were hard all over. When I was fifteen, my parents lost our family farm in the Ozark Mountains and we moved into the town of West Plains, Missouri. By the time I was in my late teens, I had a job as a butcher for Sid Vaughn's Meat Market. I loved music, and when business was slow—which was fairly often—I'd pick up my guitar and play and sing for Sid to pass the time.

Sid thought I had talent. He convinced the local radio station, KWPM, to broadcast a fifteen-minute show three days a week from the market. When Sid told me, I was terrified. But Sid thought it would be good for business, and I wanted to help out. In fact, it turned out it wasn't that bad. At the start, it was only me and Sid and the engineer, so I could pretend we were just passin' the time, as always.

The reaction was satisfying. Sid's business quadrupled within weeks. Still, I was so shy that it took three months before I felt comfortable enough to laugh out loud on the air. Who would have thought that people would notice? But they did. The local folks stopped in, or dropped a note, saying they liked my music, and I should laugh more often. Their friendly acceptance was a real boost to my confidence.

But as soon as I began to feel comfortable playing for my neighbors there in West Plains, another crisis came my way. I'd come to the attention of the folks at KWTO, the big country music station out of the city of Springfield. The station manager, Ralph Foster, offered me my own early-morning show; I would also join the entire KWTO cast on the popular noontime *Ozark Farm and Home Hour.* E. E. "Si" Simon, one of country music's legendary businessmen, offered to manage me.

I was ecstatic but terrified. Thirty-five dollars a week, just for making music? Back then, that was a lot of money, even more than I made doing "real work" at Sid's. But to leave West Plains for a big city? Could I handle it?

I did the only thing I could think of. I asked my friends and neighbors for help. "I'll be up there all by myself in the big town," I said on my last local broadcast. "Please write me if you can."

I got to Springfield on Saturday night; my first show was Monday morning at 5:30 A.M. KWTO had their own band who would back me. We only had one session on that Sunday to practice the songs I'd be singing. The band members seemed real nice; but I didn't know them and they didn't know me, yet I was expected to go on the air live with only one rehearsal.

Monday morning I was so nervous I could barely get my fingers to work. I wasn't in Sid's anymore; I was in a fancy studio with a control booth and lights that told you what to do. And this wasn't a show for my neighbors; KWTO broadcast to four states.

Well, the show started, and after the first song, my nerves felt worse than ever. So I did what I'd learned to do back in West Plains—I told the truth.

"Folks," I said, "I'm a country boy, and I sure am nervous coming to a city like this and singing. I hope you like me and my music. If you don't, drop me a line anyhow; I'd love to hear from you."

I'm sure the backup band thought I was crazy telling everybody that I was shy and nervous, but I figured they could tell anyhow and it was best to come out and be honest about it. It helped me, anyway, and the next song was a little easier to sing.

Everybody at KWTO had a little cubby mailbox, and I kept close watch on mine. Tuesday: nothing. Wednesday: empty. Thursday; I started to worry. Maybe folks *didn't* like my singing, and they were too polite to tell me so. But what could I do? There was nothing on Friday, either, and I worried about that, and my decision to come to Springfield, all weekend.

Still trying to decide what to do, I went in on Monday morning and did my show, then went across the street to the diner for breakfast. When I came back by the mail desk, the lady in charge said, "Porter, when are you going to pick up your mail?"

I said, "Well, I guess as soon as I get some."

She said, "Oh, Honey, you need to look down in the basement; you've got *boxes* of mail down there."

Well, I ran down those basement steps and there were three huge boxes—real tall and stuffed full of mail—and all of it was for me! There were thousands of letters, from people everywhere.

I was so overwhelmed that I sat down and cried, probably for ten minutes straight. It was the most touching thing that had ever happened to me in my life. Every time I'd start to get up and go upstairs, I'd start crying again to think that so many people had taken the time to encourage a kid like me.

Finally I pulled myself together because I knew I had to get ready for the noon show. I went upstairs, and as I walked past Ralph Foster's office, he hollered at me, "Hey, come in here a minute, Porter; I want to see you."

I was embarrassed because it was obvious I'd been crying, but when the station manager calls you in, you go.

Ralph said, "I guess you've seen all the mail downstairs?"

I said, "Yeah, I sure did."

He said, "Well, we've never had anybody get that much mail before in the history of this radio station. I thought you might be interested to know that we're going to start you at double what we said we would—at seventy dollars a week."

I couldn't believe it. It was all I could do to not start crying again. I stammered out my thanks and added, "I'll always try to do a good job for you."

I was just a shy country boy from West Plains, who was lucky enough to be taught early on the importance of being honest with your audience—honest with people—and not to be ashamed to be exactly who you are.

Porter Wagoner

The Dream

*I*t's *important to dream.*

Conway Twitty

We're living this story we're about to tell you. We will always be living it as long as we're alive and working together as a family.

Our daddy, Johnny Wiggins, came to Nashville in 1958 and worked odd jobs. He loved music and wanted to be in the business, but he didn't know anybody here, like so many people. What he did know was how to work on engines—he was a mechanic. So one of the jobs he finally got was with the Metropolitan Transit Authority, where he worked on buses. Daddy also made good friends with the manager of the bus company.

Ernest Tubb was one of the few touring acts that had a tour bus at the time. Back in those days, the band took turns driving the bus. When it broke down, they had to call the wrecker and get it towed in to the shop. So Ernest was the guy who came up with the idea to hire somebody to drive the bus and be able to work on it when it broke down.

One day when he was bringing the bus in to get repaired, he asked the manager to recommend someone. The manager told him about our daddy, and he got hired on the spot!

Well, what Ernest didn't know was that Daddy was trying to get into the music business when he started driving for him. After working for Ernest for a few years, Ernest found out that Daddy could sing and he started letting him open shows. He put him on the cover of the Troubadour albums and Daddy ended up getting a deal with Decca Records.

His career was just getting started, which is what he always wanted. Ernest Tubb was notorious for touring an extended amount of time. At one time, Daddy was gone fifty-two days straight.

One time, when my older sister and I were still in diapers, a cab dropped him off in front of the house. I was out playing in the driveway and I ran away from him. That's when he realized that with something he loved as much as me in his life, he would have to make a choice between the business or raising his family. So he made that decision and took us back to North Carolina, where he worked for his brothers in the paving business. It was really hard for him to leave it behind. But he never really could quite give up the music that was so deep within him.

As Audrey and I grew, he saw a talent there and he began to develop that talent. He'd let us go out and sing at private parties; he had me singing with the Troubadours when I was four; and Audrey at the Grand Ole Opry when she was twelve.

Eighteen years ago he had the idea to have us sing together as a duet. He said, "There's not a family act in country music right now. There's not a brother and sister act, so it would be great if we could get the two of you together."

After six years we finally got a record deal and things were just starting to take off. Daddy always said that he wanted to be on Mercury Records and he had a feeling that one day his kids would somehow be involved with them.

We got a deal in January of 1993. We were here in Nashville when we got the call. I had just found the song "Has Anyone Here Seen Amy" on a Friday and I was going to call Daddy on Saturday. Daddy had heard a couple of cuts on this album. We had been working on it for two years. I was going to call him that day. He and Momma were going out to dinner and I loved this song so much that I wanted Daddy's opinion on it. He died that night before I could play it for him—killed in a car wreck.

It was awful. We were finally seeing our dreams of a debut album, and he was finally seeing his dreams come true vicariously through us. And then we lost him.

So on our next album we found a song called "The Dream." It was about what we do. Working all your life and being drawn to country music because it's in your blood despite all the hardships that go along with the music business. We wanted to somehow include Daddy on this album.

On one of those old Troubadour albums, Ernest Tubb introduces Daddy at the Spanish Castle Ballroom in Seattle, Washington. Our producer took segments of that night and put it with our song called "The Dream," which brings it all full circle. Daddy always wanted to be on Mercury Records and now he finally is—with us.

John and Audrey Wiggins

The Front-Row Seats

The Bible says, "All things are possible." I believe that.

Dolly Parton

My family have always been country music fans. My mother's favorite entertainer was Porter Wagoner, and even as a little girl of five growing up in Louisiana, Momma passed that "hero worship" on to me. While all of my friends were singing Beatles tunes, I knew all the words to "Slew Foot."

One of my earliest memories was the day Porter was to perform near my hometown at the Ponchatoula Hayride. We stood in line for four hours just waiting for the doors to open so we could get a good seat. Unfortunately, hundreds of other people had the same idea, and by the time Momma made it through the rushing crowd, protecting her small daughter, we had to sit near the back of the building. Instead of being disappointed, Momma smiled at me, took my hand and said, "That's okay, baby. One of these days we're going to have front-row seats."

As fate would have it, thirty years later I was the feature

producer for the television program *Opry Backstage* on TNN. I can't begin to tell you how proud that made Momma. She had been suffering from an extended illness and died soon after I got the position. However, she died knowing I was working with the stars of her beloved Grand Ole Opry.

Shortly after her death my producer, Rusty Wilcoxen, asked me to participate in a live segment for the show. I was to be interviewed by the host of *Opry Backstage*— Porter Wagoner. During the commercial break as I was being miked and placed into position for the interview, I felt as if someone had taken my hand. No one was touching me, but the sensation was real.

As I looked at the crew in front of me, my thoughts suddenly raced to Momma, and for an instant I was the five-year-old girl again. To my left, less than a foot away, sat Momma's favorite entertainer about to talk to her only child in front of millions of viewers. A single tear trickled down my cheek. As the floor manager was counting us out of the break, I spoke to Momma. Not out loud, but from the heart.

We did it, Momma. We finally got those front-row seats! The tear was replaced by a smile.

Roxane Russell

"She said name three stars and I put
Garth Brooks, Clint Black and Alan Jackson.
What's wrong with that?"

Reprinted by permission of Martha Campbell. ©1998 Martha Campbell.

Dream Big

A dream is a wish your heart makes.

Walt Disney

My husband, Greg, and I are the parents of two daughters, Kelly, age nineteen, and Carrie, age sixteen. Kelly was born with spina bifida and hydrocephalus, birth defects that occur when the spinal column does not fully close, resulting in an "open spine." As the parent of a disabled child, one of the hardest things I have had to deal with is not being able to make all of Kelly's dreams come true.

One of Kelly's dreams was centered around country music star John Berry. Our family was first introduced to John's music through Kelly. We all watched John's music video as he performed "You and Only You," and we were inspired by the way he sang with his heart.

A loyal fan of John's, Kelly was very moved after learning about his 1994 personal challenge with brain surgery. Kelly also has a brain cyst and related strongly to John's feelings.

In 1996, our family attended six of John's concerts. That August, John signed a poster for Kelly with the words,

"Thank you for listening to my music. Dream Big." Kelly took his message to heart!

At past shows, we had watched as John came out into the audience and danced with fans. Prior to attending the September 27, 1996, concert in Penn Yan, New York, Kelly and I had one of our regular heart-to-heart talks. She told me about a dream of hers to dance with John at a concert and asked me if this might be possible. I thought for a while before I answered and then told her, "Probably not because it would be very hard for John to bend down to reach you in your wheelchair." She said she understood, but that she "could still dream."

Our family had tickets to both of John's concerts that night. Kelly, Carrie and I sat under a huge tent close to the front of the stage. Greg was seated toward the back. Near the end of the first show, Kelly held a gift of flowers in her hands. When John walked down into the audience, he came toward Kelly to accept her flowers. He then bent down and danced with her! I just sat and watched, tears running down my face. John then danced with our other daughter, Carrie. He danced with me next, and all I could say over and over was, "You will never know, but you just made my daughter's dream come true."

My husband does not usually show his emotions, but that night he cried his eyes out. At the end of the second show, John looked at Kelly and said over the microphone that he had watched her singing the words to all of his songs. He then called Carrie to the stage and gave her his guitar pick along with the song list he had taped to the stage as gifts for Kelly. We met John after the show, when everyone else had left, and we could not thank him enough.

I would like to share part of a letter I sent to John Berry in November 1996:

Our entire family has to hear you sing live again. Your voice, lyrics and very presence make us forget the reality of our lives for a short while. The memories will remain with us forever and somehow buffer our family against the next crisis that will surely come our way. You are a magical lifeline. It is a twofold blessing for me to watch what happens to Kelly as she watches you sing and as I watch her singing every song out loud with you. For that brief moment in time, I know that all of her dreams came true and her prayers were answered. For a mother, there is no greater reward. My thanks to you, John.

Rita Batts

Inspired by Love

Always know in your heart that you are far bigger than anything that can happen to you.

Dan Zadra

As early as I can remember, I craved being in the spotlight. When I was two, I would crowd my mom and dad and aunt, uncles and cousins into our living room at holidays and sing them songs. The desire grew stronger throughout my childhood and became my life's ambition.

I was blessed to have two of the most loving and supportive parents a child could have. It was this warm, adoring encouragement that helped so much when an electric floor fan fell over on me and I lost the little finger on my left hand. I was thirteen months old, and I don't even remember it happening. I think it was as traumatic for my parents as it was for me, but they handled it beautifully. Even though they knew losing my finger was going to be a challenge, they also knew my love of music would conquer any obstacles that I encountered.

When I turned four, they decided to start me on piano lessons. Once a week, I packed my piano books under my arm and cheerfully walked up the street and around the corner in our Florida Gulf Coast town to the home of Irene Market, my piano teacher. Mrs. Market was elderly, small and frail—a wisp of a woman. But oh! That wisp could fill your heart with inspiration and make your fingers dance. She loved music, and she loved children. She made me love piano.

There was only one problem. When I started lessons playing "Hot Cross Buns," I did fine practicing on one of those little pianos like Schroeder plays in "Peanuts," but after a couple of years, when it became clear that I had a talent for piano and wanted to continue—it also became obvious that I'd outgrown my "baby grand."

That made for a new problem. My mom and dad were both public school teachers. Dad was a painter who taught high school art, and Mom taught home economics; and they both loved their work. However, their salaries just didn't provide enough money to buy a real piano.

Then one day I got the surprise of my young life. Mom and Dad called me out into the garage. There, big as life, was a brown upright piano. Squealing with delight, I pulled the bench over and began playing. All those keys! They went on and on for octaves, and all but the highest key and the lowest key worked.

When I asked where it came from, Mom grinned and said she'd found it at a garage sale—for twenty-five dollars.

"It doesn't look like much now," she said. "But I'll take care of that."

I can still picture how scratched and battered the wood of that old piano was. But true to her word and her creativity, within days, Mom had covered that piano with contact paper. It had orange and green mushrooms on it. For a kid in the late sixties, that was the height of cool.

The arrival of that piano began a new era in my life. It lived in the garage, which was where my dad had his "art studio" set. To this day, I remember the glorious sounds and smells of creativity—oil paint, plaster, canvas and even the oil leaking from under the car. From then on I lived in the garage. It became my own personal stage. I sang and danced on the grandest stages in front of huge audiences, and I didn't even have to close my eyes. I lived in a continuous musical, like a daydream, performing alongside such stars as Judy Garland, who inspired me so much as the child star of the *Wizard of Oz.*

From my old piano, I learned that music defined much of who I was and what I loved. Practicing for hours every day was a joy. And the old piano gave its all. Being in the garage, the instrument was subjected to Gulf Coast weather year-round—through the humidity of summer and the cold of winter. (Yes, there are some cold winters in Florida!) Sometimes during the winter, I'd take a bowl of steaming water out with me, and when my fingers got too cold to continue, I'd warm them in the water and play on. Of course, our house became a regular stop on the piano tuner's rounds.

Not everyone was supportive, and the magic didn't always occur. In college, I prepared to sing an aria from the opera *Tales of Hoffman.* When my name was called, I said a quick prayer and walked onstage to face the audience— and the panel of judges. My voice was in fine form for the occasion, and I felt really good as I gestured with my hands to accent the lyrics. Afterward, as the audience warmly applauded my performance, I felt a wonderful glow of satisfaction. From the smile on the faces of the judges, I was confident they had enjoyed the piece as well.

Out in the hallway, I ran into the vocal professor. She stopped me and said, "I saw your performance, and I have to say . . ." She hesitated. "I was really distracted by your missing finger. You need to rework your movements so that your hand isn't so visible. It's really disturbing."

This is where I have to give my parents so much credit. Because of their nurturing and constant encouragement, I've never felt like I had a handicap at all. I believe that God gave me a voice and musical talent to share with others, to make them feel good, and I believe he gave me the challenge of my childhood mishap to encourage others, to let them know that they have more strength than they sometimes realize. He's also given me this wonderful career in country music—a lifelong dream come true. Looking back, I can never recall the insensitive music professor's words without remembering the old piano. I'm sure by the time the piano reached the garage sale, its owners saw a battered hunk of worthless junk. Maybe they could get twenty-five dollars for it. I admit that green and orange mushrooms might not add a lot to the value *these* days. But if you were willing to look past the outer imperfections, inside that piano was a magical world of beautiful music—and the promise of possibilities for a young girl.

Lari White
As told by Ron Camacho

A Cowboy's Last Chance

Joe Wimberly sat on a tree stump and stared at his house. It sits on a skinny road that meanders out of Cool, Texas, population 238, a flat, dusty place without so much as a drugstore or a gas station.

"It ain't exactly the Ponderosa," Joe once told his wife, Paula, as he swept his arm toward the three acres or so of scrub grass that went with the little house. "But it's our ranch."

Joe wore a cowboy hat and sported a bushy black mustache that matched his eyes, as dark as Texas oil. He was missing a tooth, right on the fifty-yard line. But his jaw was square and strong. And he stood taller than his five-foot-five-inch frame.

Earlier that day, Joe received a call from the banker, who wanted money. The charge cards were full, the payments were late, the checking account was overdrawn. Joe didn't have a nickel to his name, except for the house. And he swore he would never let that go.

Being a cowboy was all Joe Wimberly knew. He had learned to ride a horse by the time he was four. At seven, he was herding cattle with his father. At thirteen, he was climbing onto the back of a steer.

When Joe turned eighteen, he set out for a world where the Old West still lives, the last untamed range for the true American cowboy—the rodeo. Soon, anybody who knew rodeo came to know the name of Joe Wimberly. There were days when he walked around with one thousand dollars in his pocket. Other times he could not afford to eat. But there was never a day when he wanted to trade his chaps for a job with a boss looking over his shoulder.

It scared Paula to watch Joe on a bull. Still, she knew being a cowboy put the sparkle in his eyes, and she never wanted to see that fade. So whenever he headed out the door, she kissed him good-bye, crossed her fingers and said a prayer.

Joe was gone to the rodeo about two hundred days a year. He was one thousand miles away on the night Paula gave birth to a daughter, Casey. They had no insurance. "How we gonna pay for things, Joe?" Paula's voice cracked across the telephone wires.

"I'm gonna win," Joe told her. "And I'm gonna keep winning."

He was as good as his word. With the grace of a gymnast and the nerve of a bank robber, Joe dazzled crowds at little county fairs and big city stadiums throughout the West. In the 1980s he qualified five times to compete in the National Finals Rodeo. In his best year, Joe won more than eighty thousand in prize money.

However, with travel expenses and entry fees ranging from twenty-five dollars to more than three hundred dollars, times were never easy, especially after the birth of another daughter, Sami. But bills got paid, and when Paula took a job in a pharmacy, they saved enough for a down payment on their house.

Joe could already envision a place for a horse corral on what was now the Wimberly Ranch. He poured a cement slab near the back door, then took a tree twig and carved the names of the Wimberly clan in the cement. Shortly after, Paula gave birth to a son, McKennon.

Even when he was hurt, Joe seldom missed a rodeo. Once, his wrist got caught in the rope, and he dangled on the side of the bull as it kicked him and knocked him unconscious. He was taken away on a stretcher, blood running down his face.

He came back from that injury and many others. But by now weeks had passed since he'd brought home a paycheck. *Maybe I'm just not trying hard enough,* Joe thought. The bills were all way past due.

Mesquite, on the outskirts of Dallas, is the site of one of the best-known rodeos in America. One day a Dodge Truck executive called rodeo owner Neal Gay with a promotion idea. If Gay would pick the meanest, wildest bull he could find, Dodge would put up a five-thousand-dollar prize for any cowboy who could ride it for eight seconds. The pot would grow by five hundred dollars every time the bull shucked a rider. The bull would be named after a new truck, Dodge Dakota.

Gay liked the idea. He contacted Lester Meier, a rodeo producer who owned a nightmarish black bull that weighed 1,700 pounds and had a single horn crawling ominously down the side of its white face.

"You got your Dodge Dakota," Meier told Gay.

Of the thirty bull riders who competed at Mesquite every weekend, only one, assigned randomly by a computer, got a crack at Dodge Dakota. Week after week, the beast sent cowboys hurtling, even a former world champion. But Joe Wimberly was never chosen.

Joe was carrying a fifty-pound feed sack toward the horse pen at his ranch when he heard the screen door slam. Paula hurried over. "The rodeo called, Joe," she said. "You drew Dodge Dakota for Friday night."

Joe dropped the feed sack. "You're kiddin' me."

"No, Joe, I ain't kiddin'." The pot had grown to $9,500.

Joe started riding the bull in his mind. *Stay loose,* he told himself. *This is just another bull.* But Joe knew Dakota was a vicious outlaw.

According to those who had studied Dakota, the bull started every ride the same way. It blew out of the chute, took one jump, kicked over its head, stepped backward and spun to the left, all in about two seconds. After that, it was anybody's guess.

That Friday, Joe paced behind the chutes. He looked up in the stands and saw his family. When the spotlight flashed on him, he pulled himself over the rails and settled on the broad, humped back of Dodge Dakota. He wrapped the rope around his right hand; the other end was twisted around the belly of the beast.

Lord, I'm comin' to you like a friend, Joe pleaded silently. *You know how much I need this ride.* Beads of sweat grew on his forehead.

The gate swung open. Dakota bolted, and Joe's thighs squeezed tight. The beast bucked hard, lifting Joe into the air, then slammed down. The bull bellowed and twisted to its left. Foam spewed from its snout. The cowboy thumped back on his seat, the rope burning his hand. He shot in the air, his head snapping backward, hat flying off, but he hung on. The stands thundered—six thousand fans on their feet, screaming, shrieking, stomping. The clock flashed five seconds, six seconds . . .

Dakota groaned in a voice from hell and bucked violently, four hoofs in the air. Suddenly the bull ran alone.

Crashing flat on his back, Joe looked up to see the belly of the bull and its slamming hoofs. He scrambled away as the clowns chased Dakota back to its pen. Joe searched for Paula in the stands and slowly mouthed the words, "I am sorry."

Later that summer, Joe was again paired with Dodge Dakota. In an instant this time, the bull slammed him and his dreams to dirt.

Now Joe was scrambling for money. He shod horses. He entered jackpot bull-riding contests, organized a rodeo school. But none of this put much of a dent in his debts. He was finally forced to place an ad in the house-for-sale section of the newspaper. "It's only boards and paint and siding," he told a tearful Paula. "If we stay together as a family, it doesn't matter where we are."

Joe paid another humiliating visit to the banker. "Can't I have just a little more time?" the cowboy pleaded.

"You've had time, Joe," the banker said flatly.

One Friday in September, Joe was riding at Mesquite. With all his troubles at home, Joe hadn't been thinking much about bulls. The purse for Dodge Dakota had grown to seventeen thousand dollars.

They had stopped announcing ahead of time which cowboy would ride Dakota. Now they drew the name during intermission. Suddenly a rodeo official called out, "Hey, Joe Wimberly, you got Dakota."

Neal Gay came by. "Third time's the charm," the rodeo owner said with a wink.

As Paula watched from the stands, her heart began to pound. Twice before, she had seen Joe's hopes soar as high as the stars, and then sink to the depths.

Joe climbed up to the bucking chutes. The season was almost over. Twenty-four times a cowboy had boarded Dodge Dakota, and twenty-four times the bull had won. The pot was big enough to save his house, to pay the bills, even to have a little extra.

The cowboy pulled himself over the rails and straddled the bull that stomped inside its chute. The rope was wrapped around his hand as tight as a noose. One of his favorite phrases came to mind: "If you ain't got no choice, be brave."

The gate swung open, and the clock started counting the eight most important seconds of Joe Wimberly's life.

The huge black beast bellowed. Nearly a ton of muscle and bone thundered by. Dakota's head snapped violently. Its eyes flashed fire. Dust rose from its kicking hoofs. And the clock ticked—two seconds . . . three . . . four . . .

Joe bounced on the bull's hard back, straining for balance. Then another punishing buck. He dangled at the edge, fighting gravity. Six seconds . . . seven seconds . . .

Joe crashed to the dirt as the horn sounded. A sudden hush swept over the arena. The fans stared down at the rodeo boss, who was staring at the timekeeper, who was staring at the clock.

An excited official raised his arms in the air, the sign of a touchdown. Joe had made it by two-hundredths of a second.

The cowboy dropped to his knees. "Thank you, Jesus!" Joe cried.

Paula fell sobbing into the arms of a spectator. The two girls sprinted down the stairs of the grandstands, while McKennon screamed, "Daddy did it! Daddy did it!"

From his knees, Joe looked up and met Paula's eyes as she ran toward him. The roar of the crowd swept down on the arena floor, where the Wimberly family squeezed together in a ten-armed hug, their tears spilling on the dust.

It was past 2 A.M. when they got home. Joe went to the telephone and dialed the banker. "Who's this!" came a groggy mumble.

"Why, this here is Joe Wimberly," he said, "and I was just calling to say I got a check for you."

Dirk Johnson

Big House

Do what you love, the money will follow.

Marsha Sinetar

My partner, David Neuhauser, and I have been playing together on and off for twenty years. When we decided to make a boom-box recording of our new songs, we were living in a big house in Van Nuys, California, rehearsing with the band. The next day, our keyboard player came over with the tape we recorded and said, "You guys have *got* to listen to this!"

It was *magic*. Dave and I just looked at each other and said, "*This* is what we've been waiting for."

For years, I would come to Bakersfield and play with whatever country band Dave had going. We were too country for rock'n'roll in our early days. We were also too bluesy for country or too country for the blues audience. But every time I came and sat in with Dave, the same thing would happen—over and over—the crowd would go nuts and we'd have a ball. We would do these great country songs and put a blues twist to them, just for fun. Many nights, we'd be sitting there after a gig and Dave would say, "We've got to go to Nashville."

I always had the same reply, "Are you kidding? Those cats in Nashville won't get it."

Dave would also always mention another name along with the conversation of Nashville, and that was Tony Brown, President of MCA records. Dave said, "*He'd* get what we do." And I just thought my partner was nuts all those years.

The whole Big House story got started at a place called "Trout's." This bar is over forty years old and plays live country music seven nights a week. It's the place where Merle Haggard and Buck Owens got started. The town is actually Oildale, a suburb of Bakersfield. Oildale isn't where the people who *own* the oil wells live; it's where the people who *work* the wells live. It was a tough crowd, but they knew their country music. A typical comment would be, "You're aw'right son, but you ain't no Merle Haggard."

Finally, we got an opportunity to play the Blue Bird Cafe in Nashville. We traveled there in a minivan. You can imagine what six big guys and their gear looked like in this small van! We drove on East with our feet in each other's noses. When we got to the Blue Bird, we didn't think anyone would show. We were surprised when quite a few did; and we got a standing ovation.

So we came back to California and told our manager, Robbie Randall, that things went *great* in Nashville. At the time, we were making a tape of the things we did and thought maybe we'd make a record and release it ourselves.

On our second trip to Nashville, we played the Ace of Clubs. We still didn't know what would happen or who would show up. A buzz had started in town about the tape we'd made. We were lucky to have volunteer advance men help us out—people like Merlin Littlefield, former Associate Director of ASCAP Publishing. Merlin would drive around Nashville with his top down, tape turned up, and pull people over. So when we got to the

Ace of Clubs, everyone in town showed up. There were *ten* record labels there that night and a packed house. We put on a whale of a show!

Before we got halfway back to California, we had offers. About the only record company that didn't show up at the Ace of Clubs in Nashville was MCA Records. As soon as we got back to Bakersfield, Tony Brown of MCA Records called up saying he wanted to see the band. He flew out to Los Angeles to meet with us. He even paid for a private rehearsal room at SIR Studios. Considering we were flat broke when we returned, that was a real blessing.

So we had this private showcase—on a big stage—in this big room—for an audience of just two people, MCA's Tony Brown and Larry Willoughby. Not the most comfortable situation for any band! Luckily my car had already been stolen that day, so I wasn't worried about a little thing like a private audition for two major recording executives.

We started off with our hit, "Cold Outside." About three songs into the showcase, the president of MCA Los Angeles, Jay Boberg, came in and Tony Brown stopped us. "Play that song, 'Cold Outside,' again. I really dig that song." That broke the ice; we just cut loose and did what we did every night. After we got done, Tony said, "I want to sign you to MCA." It was pretty overwhelming. He not only signed us, he released the demo tape we had made. We're the only band that's ever done that on MCA. He didn't change a thing! It was a dream come true to coproduce our own record with Peter Bunetta and have Tony give us the freedom to just set up, dial up some great guitar tones, and do it live.

This has been a fantastic year! We've been out touring with *everybody*—Collin Raye, Patty Loveless, Merle Haggard, Blackhawk, Dwight Yoakam, Travis Tritt, Leroy Parnell and many others—we've been treated great. We're the number-one selling new band in country in 1997, and we'll be heading back to Europe soon where we're also doing real well.

Staying the course and being true to the roots of the music you make is like having a family identity. What we have always wanted to do—and finally are doing—is bringing everyone into the Big House.

Monty Byrom

5

OVERCOMING OBSTACLES AND HARDSHIPS

If you want the rainbow, you've got to put up with a little rain.

Dolly Parton

Just Keep Walking

When I was growing up in Georgia, I loved to sing and play the guitar, even though I had no illusions about being especially skilled at either one. I was pretty gun-shy about performing in public, but I knew I wanted a career in country music. I figured if I couldn't make it on stage, maybe I could succeed as a songwriter. In 1977, I moved to Nashville to pursue that dream. When the music community didn't immediately embrace me, as I had hoped they would, I was forced to take a day job as a desk clerk at a motel to support my family. Naturally, that didn't leave much time for writing songs.

To make matters worse, within a couple of years, I began to lose my eyesight, due to complications from diabetes. By 1980, the doctors said they could do no more; I was totally blind. After receiving the news that I'd never see again, I went through months and months of depression and soul searching. During that period I spent most of my time just lying in bed day and night. Some days it took a real effort to get up and get dressed before my wife came home from work, but I didn't want her to know how defeated I felt.

I had a friend, Judy Mahaffey, another aspiring songwriter, who I would talk to several times a week by telephone. One day she asked me a really strange question, "Is your garbage can full?"

Startled, I said, "I have no idea. Why?"

"Go check," she answered. I went into the kitchen and discovered it was full. When I reported that to Judy, she simply said, "Take it out."

"What do you mean take it out? Judy, I'm blind. How am I supposed to get to the Dumpster?"

"You'll figure it out," was all she said.

That turned into a real adventure. I picked up the trash and carried it about fifty yards across the apartment complex parking lot. I was real tentative and took little tiny baby steps, but I finally got going. I'd take a step, bang into something, get scared, gather my resolve and move on. Finally, I made it to the Dumpster. By the time I got there, I felt like I'd climbed Mount Olympus. That was the moment things started to turn around.

Within a few weeks after I emptied the trash on my own, I set up a training session with a mobility instructor. She taught me to walk using a cane to guide myself. She also introduced me to the bus system.

Using the bus to return to Music Row, I developed a relationship with Pi-Gem Music, a publishing company who didn't offer me any money, but did provide me with office space. Every day for the next two years, hot or cold, rain or shine, I made the trek to my office to write songs.

Unbeknownst to me, a fellow named Chuck Neese, who had an office across the street from Pi-Gem, was watching the whole time. He told me years later that he often wondered who that blind man was. He said that he figured that I must want to be a songwriter real bad and that I was the kind of guy he'd like to work with if he ever got the chance.

One afternoon, right after Chuck had taken over as head of Alabama's new publishing company, we ran into each other. His first question was, "Who are you and what do you do?"

"I'm trying to be a songwriter," I answered.

Chuck said he wanted to hear some of my stuff, so the next day I went over to his office. The second song I played was "Nobody But You," which after being recorded by country superstar Don Williams, turned out to be my first number one record.

Over the next few years a number of other hits followed by such artists as Alabama, the Forester Sisters and John Schneider. As those records were climbing the charts, however, further complications from the diabetes surfaced. Having lost the use of my eyes, my kidneys were the next organs to be affected. In turn, this impacted my overall health. Along with my health, my songwriting, my marriage, my finances, and my emotional stability all started heading down the tubes. I was as low as I had ever been, feeling lost and uncertain. It wasn't until the spring of 1989 that I experienced another life-changing event.

One morning, for reasons I still can't explain, I didn't feel like going to the office. I was planning to write at home that day and I decided to go for a walk to clear my head before I got started. I asked my wife to drop me off on Music Row and began hoofing it back home. Within a couple of blocks, I accidentally caught the tip of my aluminum cane under a bus bench and snapped it completely in two.

I was pretty upset about this turn of events but I realized I could just have a seat on the bench and wait for one of my friends who customarily travel that area on their way to work to rescue me. Before I sat down, I heard a voice inside me clearly direct me to, "Just keep walking."

The words repeated themselves the instant I questioned them; so I reluctantly obeyed. At first, it was difficult to trust the process, but after a few blocks, walking without my cane felt perfectly natural—natural, at least until I approached a major intersection.

When I hesitated, I heard the voice again advising me, "Just keep walking, son, you're doing fine." After I made it across six lanes of traffic, I began to feel so comfortable that I even refused a ride from a friend who stopped alongside. She later told me I looked so relaxed that she hadn't noticed I didn't have my cane.

As I moved along, I couldn't get over how good I felt, serene in the feeling that everything was going to be all right. I felt at peace about that walk and about my life in general. It was really strange knowing I should be scared but I wasn't. I can't explain it, but I felt completely taken care of.

I wish I could tell you that my life worked out perfectly after that; but it hasn't been quite that simple. My marriage could not be salvaged. A difficult divorce and financial distress followed. My career bottomed out. My health continued to suffer culminating in complete kidney failure and more than a year of difficult dialysis treatments. Through it all, however, I was able in my mind to return to that walk and hear that reassuring voice telling me to "Just keep walking."

I walked a long way before the situation turned around, but when it did, it did so in a mighty way. Kidney and pancreas transplants eliminated the need for dialysis and insulin injections and my career rebounded with eight more hits, including six number-one records.

In 1991, I attended a codependency workshop, On-Sight, in South Dakota. My group counselor, Ted Klontz, was incredibly supportive and has become a friend for life.

At the end of the treatment program, Ted and my fellow group members outlined how they'd seen me develop and grow. They also made a recommendation that I reconnect with my musical side by performing in public.

Remembering my insecurities as a teenager, I totally rejected the idea. When I got back to Nashville, however, I felt myself being led in that direction by the same voice that had kept me moving several years earlier. Little by little, I began playing writer's nights in small clubs around town, quickly discovering a lot of joy and fulfillment in my music again.

My roller-coaster ride continued over the next few years with some really terrible things and some really wonderful things. In late September, 1995, my transplanted kidney failed. In October of that same year, I married Janet, my soul mate, my best friend, and the love of my life. In March of 1997, circulation problems caused by the diabetes resulted in a below the knee amputation of my right leg. Four months later, I got another kidney transplant, but in September I was back in the hospital for the amputation of my left leg.

The trials seemed to go hand in hand with the triumphs but through it all I just kept walking and my dreams kept coming true.

Working with the Nashville office of the American Diabetes Association, I teamed up with several other writers and performers to produce a pair of concerts that raised over eighty thousand dollars for diabetes education and research. We performed at the Ryman Auditorium, the venerable home of the Grand Ole Opry. For me, it was the culmination of yet another dream. Ted Klontz, my On-Sight counselor, and his wife Margie, flew into town for the first of those occasions. Their presence and that performance reminded me just how much change is possible in one person's life. In less than five years, I had gone from saying, "I'll play in public when hell freezes over," to playing a show at the mother church of country music with Waylon Jennings, Hal Ketchum and Rodney Crowell—all heroes of mine.

With the loss of both my legs, a transplanted kidney and the use of my eyes, I've come to realize something quite remarkable. I'm more than just my body. Through all the trauma, my life has continued undisturbed at a much, much deeper level. Now don't get the idea any of the physical changes have been easy to accept. They haven't. I've often lashed out, demanding that God put an end to all the catastrophe. I'm finally coming to accept, however, that there are no guarantees for any of us, about anything, but I have choices about whether or not the fear and frustration go as deep as my soul. So far, thank God, my soul is intact and as long as that's the case, I'll pay attention when he tells me to "Just keep walking."

John Jarrard

The Gift of Dignity

There are some things you learn best in calm, and some in storm.

Willa Cather

My father and mother, Kirby and Estelle Bowman, were cotton mill workers. In Alabama there used to be a great many Avondale textile mills where a lot of the local people worked. Momma and Daddy were full-time farmers as well. But Daddy only grew cotton for a year; you couldn't eat it or put it in a fruit jar, so he didn't raise it anymore. There were ten of us children in the family, with two or three years separating us in age. While we always had a lot of food to eat, there were very few frills in our lives. Being a big family with a meager income meant that mother sewed our clothes from Purina feed sacks: the cotton sacks that feed for cows was packaged in. Momma never had a pattern to go by. She'd get her measurements by holding the material up to our bodies, and then she'd sit down at the sewing machine and whip up a dress or shirt.

Back in those days it was left up to us kids to get a Christmas tree and decorate it. Sometimes we'd cut down a pine tree—there weren't many cedars in our part of the country—and then we'd color paper strips and glue them together to make chains to put on the tree. We never had any store-bought decorations that I can remember. Once the paper chains were on the tree we'd add red berries, or anything that we could find with some color to it. A couple of folks who were regular visitors to our home happened to be cigar smokers. They smoked cigars that came wrapped in little gold-colored bands. So we used those bands for decorations. We used anything that had some shine.

The best Christmas I could remember could have been my worst, had I let it. I've never told this story before. Even my children will be surprised to read it. Earlier, I mentioned Purina feed sacks. When you say "feed sacks," most people think of rough, heavy burlap. But these sacks were made from a printed cotton fabric of excellent quality, like the material you'd buy in a store. I think Purina was the first to package feed in this manner. It may have been an ingenious marketing idea: If a farmer bought several sacks of feed packaged in similar fabric, there would be enough material to make a garment of some kind.

The Christmas I was thirteen my gift was a new dress which Momma had made from feed sacks. The print was of small yellow daisies spread across a cream-colored background. It had a gathered skirt, round collar and puff sleeves with little bands. The sashes on each side tied into a bow at the back. It wasn't an elegant pattern, but I sure didn't think it looked like it had once been a feed sack. And so, that first morning after Christmas vacation, I climbed onto the school bus feeling very stylish in my new dress. Determined that it wouldn't get wrinkled, I found an empty seat and spread the skirt out carefully. Then I sat back, certain that I was the envy of every girl.

As was customary with a country school bus, it stopped at neighboring farms along the way to pick up the schoolchildren. At one of these farms a boy got on board. I'll never forget what happened next. I looked up and saw that he was wearing a shirt made from the same print as my dress: small yellow daisies on a cream-colored background. Then I thought I would surely die, because a girl stood up at the front of the bus and said, very loudly, "Jeanne is saving you a seat at the back. You'll fit right in." I knew this girl. She was always doing something to attract attention to herself. I don't know if she ever realized how much she hurt our feelings. When I think back on it, she was probably as poor as a church mouse, just like the rest of us.

The boy never said anything. But our eyes met as he moved toward my seat. We were both thinking the same thing: *Everybody knows we're wearing feed sacks.* He sat down next to me. When I looked over, I saw tears running down his face. They were running down my face, too. But we never spoke. Poor kids don't have to talk about being poor.

How could this be my best Christmas ever? I'll tell you how. This was the day that I decided that I would never let what other people say hurt my feelings. You might consider it a Christmas present that I gave *myself* that year. I had all day to think about what happened, and the truth was quite simple. My mother had made that Christmas dress, and she worked long, hard hours. She wasn't just a farm wife and mother to ten children; she was a working woman, too. If she wasn't at her mill job, she was in the kitchen or the garden. If she wasn't sewing or cooking, she was shelling peas, or breaking beans, or milking cows and getting the milk cooled down for the children to drink. My mother had made the dress. So, when I got home from school, I thanked her for it. I told her how pretty everyone thought it was, but I never, ever told her the truth about how much I had hurt. And from that day forward the feed sack dress became my favorite. Wherever I went, I wore it proudly. I would give anything in the world if that little dress were in my possession today.

Momma and Daddy have passed away. I guess that when the holiday season rolls around, we all find ourselves thinking of the loved ones we've lost. My mother was seventy-five years old when she died. Daddy was seventy-seven. If they were still alive, Momma would be ninety-four, and Daddy would be ninety-one. This is amazing to me. This is how time can get away, without your realizing it. In my mind, I still see them vibrant as ever, sitting under the peach trees, peeling peaches, canning vegetables and putting them away for winter. In my memory they will always be hardworking country people, doing the best they could with every day God sent them.

I've received many expensive Christmas gifts in the years since I've left Pell City, Alabama. Often, when I'm in my dressing room at the Grand Ole Opry, getting ready for a show, I think of that day on the school bus and the feed sack dress with its little puff sleeves. It doesn't matter how many elegant designer dresses or how many fabulous stage outfits I might wear; when I take them off, I can still put myself right back in that seat on that old school bus. And I realize that, but for the grace of God, I could still be there. And then I think of that boy, standing there in the shirt his own mother had sewn for him, most likely as a Christmas gift. I wonder what ever happened to him. Maybe he's a doctor now. Or a lawyer, or a farmer, like his daddy would've been. Over the years I've tried to remember his name, but it's lost to me. Wherever he is, whatever profession he chose, I hope that he's been happy, and that life has treated him well. And I hope that when he got off the school bus that day, he got off carrying what I did: the gift of dignity.

Jeanne Pruett

Excerpted from *A Country Music Christmas* by Cathie Pelletier. Copyright ©1996 by Cathie Pelletier. Reprinted by permission of Crown Publishers, Inc.

"They want to feature us on
'Lifestyles of the Rural and Repossessed.'"

Zell and Fuzz

This is a true story. It happened up in my hometown of Young Harris. Young Harris is a very small town. We didn't even have a fire department.

One day, a house caught fire. The whole town gathered around to watch it. We were helpless to put it out. About that time, we saw a pickup truck come over the ridge. It was a local character named Fuzz Chastain. He had his wife with him, all their kids, a cousin or two, and some aunts and uncles.

Fuzz drove right down to where we were all standing, but he didn't stop. He drove that pickup right into the middle of the fire. He jumped out and so did everybody else. They started beating the fire with anything they could find—even their clothes.

It took 'em thirty minutes, but danged if they didn't put out that fire. The mayor of Young Harris was there. He said, "This is the most courageous thing I have ever seen in Young Harris. Let's pass the hat for Fuzz Chastain."

They raised seventeen dollars. The mayor presented the money to Fuzz. "Fuzz," he said, "the people of Young Harris appreciate this heroic act of yours." Fuzz's hair was singed, his clothes were burned and torn.

"But, Fuzz, there is one thing I'd like to know," the mayor went on. "What are you going to do with the money?"

Fuzz thought for a minute and then said, "Well, Mr. Mayor, I guess the first thing I ought to do is get the brakes fixed on that pickup."

Zell Miller
As told to Lewis Grizzard

Tyler

Someone once told me that they believed special needs children are angels God sends to us to help with our spiritual and emotional growth. Of course, I didn't always believe this was true.

After my son Tyler was born with Down's syndrome, I felt such a sense of anger and loss. I was devastated. I remember thinking, *How could I have something imperfect?* I was just so hurt. I had heard of Down's syndrome and thought it was the end of the world. I was angry at God for allowing this to happen to my child and to me. Then I felt guilty for being angry at God. There was also this incredible loss, almost a grieving for the loss of dreams a parent has for his child.

You're proud of all your kids, but with Tyler it's special because any small thing he does is a giant step. He learns so slowly, so anything he does is like "Wow, look at what Tyler's doing!"

During this difficult time, several people came into my life who really helped me to put acceptance and joy back into living. I'm not even sure they realized how important the things they said were to me. One particular comment from a friend really stands out in my mind. He said, "Joe,

I promise you that this child will bring you as much or more joy than your other children do now. Every milestone, every small accomplishment he makes will be a cause for celebration."

Tyler underwent surgery in 1991 to remove his tonsils and nearly died of asphyxiation. He was in intensive care for seven days with all these bandages on him and tubes sticking out of every portal. We almost lost him.

All the things I took for granted with my other kids— like walking, talking, eating independently, catching a ball and just being able to play—became sources of pride and cause for hope with Tyler. He may not ever be able to be president of the United States, play professional football, or even speak clearly or be able to live independently, but Tyler can give the most precious gifts of smiles and hugs and unconditional love. I guess God really does send us angels from time to time.

Joe Diffie

God Bless the U.S.A.

It was time for me to come forward and sing, with the newly revised video of "God Bless the U.S.A." flickering on the enormous screen behind me. Medals commemorating our space heroes and the men we've lost in battle had been pinned on my white jacket, which has U.S.A. emblazoned down each sleeve. I glanced out into the vast expanse of upturned faces.

Out there among the sea of military notables was a remarkable lady. Major Rhonda Leah Cornum, an army flight surgeon, had been released with the other POWs early in March. She had walked down the plane's ramp with both arms in slings, evidence of the grinding crash that she had been lucky to survive. Major Cornum had served with the 229th Battalion out of Fort Rucker. In Saudi Arabia, they were attached to the 101st Aviation Brigade, and she was always eager to volunteer for any duty whenever it came up. The airmen she worked with respected her courage and ability, considering her one of their own. Among themselves, they called her "Doc Cornum," and there were times when they were plenty worried about her safety.

Then one night an F-16 was shot down by antiaircraft

guns over Iraqi territory. The pilot was reporting his position as his plane headed in. Suddenly an explosion told the listening pilots that he was down.

"There's a chance that he got out," they hoped. A search and rescue crew was needed in case the pilot was alive. As usual, the major was quick to volunteer. So she climbed aboard the Black Hawk, a lift helicopter that transports personnel and equipment, and headed with the SAR team for the downed aviator.

As the Black Hawk reached deep behind enemy lines, volleys of shots flew up from the dark sand drifts below.

"We're taking heavy fire!" the chopper's pilot called out.

There was a short silence, then a deafening *boom!*

The helicopter had careened headfirst into the rock-strewn desert sand. Its fuselage crumbled, cracking almost completely in half.

"We've got a Hawk down!" shouted one of the pilots who was monitoring the ongoing battle.

Information was sketchy as the word filtered back to the 220th and the 101st. Her comrades were concerned about the whole crew, but mostly they worried about the major.

"Doc's down! Doc Cornum's down in Iraq!"

"Man! She's got no business being behind enemy lines!"

"She shouldn't be out there. But she's the type that'd do anything . . . so gung ho." It was spoken almost like a rebuke from a friend who felt especially protective.

"Doc volunteers for everything!" her buddies agreed, afraid that this was one dangerous mission too many for their friend.

Then a report came back: "Looks like nobody made it."

"Oh God! SAR better get out there!"

When rescue planes did get to the crash site, they found an appalling sight. The bodies of five crew members were strewn near the remnants of their crushed Black Hawk. But there was no sign of the other three.

The SAR team started searching through the wreckage.

"Their flight gear's here!" yelled one of them. "It's intact! And there's no blood! They've *got* to be alive!"

After rummaging through the debris, he said, "And someone's gone through the first-aid kit! They must have been taken by the Iraqis, but we can't be sure."

After identifying the bodies of those who were killed in action, military officials listed Major Cornum as one of the three who had vanished, an MIA. Americans who had been shocked with the capture of our first female POW, Army Specialist Melissa Rathbun-Nealy, felt the uneasiness of knowing that Saddam's forces were, in all probability, holding another of our military women.

With the abrupt end to the war, it was a relief to see our POWs set free, and we were overjoyed to learn that Major Cornum and the other two crew members from the Black Hawk were among them. The returning POWs were in better condition than we had feared. When a reporter asked the army doctor, "How did you hold up during your ordeal?" she answered, "I held up fine until we were coming home on the plane. I had heard about the video for the troops, and I was worried that when they played 'God Bless the U.S.A.,' I wouldn't be able to keep it together."

That night in our "Welcome Home, America" audience, Major Rhonda Cornum's head tilted forward as the words of the song floated out into the hall and ABC's cameras caught her lightly brushing aside the tears.

"And I won't forget the men who died who gave that right to me."

Over 140 allied personnel were killed in the Persian Gulf. In comparison to other wars, the number is small. But, on a personal level, just one casualty is a very great sacrifice.

"And I'd gladly stand up next to you and defend her still today. . . ."

The cymbals clashed, and with the words "stand up," it seemed as though everyone in the whole audience rose to their feet. I looked out on a sea of faces and, by the reflected glow of the stage lights, saw thousands of forms tightly holding hands, their arms raised high above their heads.

"'Cause there ain't no doubt I love this land—"

My clenched fist hit my chest, then struck the air above my head.

"God bless the U.S.A."

Then I called out to the standing, cheering crowd, "Do you feel the pride?"

Shrill whistles and shouts of "Yeah!" answered my question.

Then, walking across the stage, I continued, "Our servicemen and women are here tonight—and are out there at home along with the rest of the nation, watching this tribute to our champions of freedom. And I want them to see some of the faces in tonight's audience.

"Sing it with me, one more time!" Then glancing back at the band I asked, "Guys, would you help me?"

"And I'm proud to be an American, where at least I know I'm free."

As this final chorus rang out again, taking over the evening, everyone rose to their feet again, searching for the words, their arms still reaching upward. The moment glowed with their exhilaration to be cheering an American triumph. I jumped down from the stage and began walking through the aisle, out into the midst of the singing military men and women, while they swayed to the drum's strong cadence.

"Come on, y'all!" I urged.

One after another, voices joined in, singing with soft timidity at first, then increasing in volume until they sounded out with conviction and pride.

"And I won't forget the men who died who gave that right to me."

Because of sacrifices in the past and the people in the emerging democracies who are demanding their individual freedom, this world is changing fast. The will to be free persists. America has founded a legacy that will be victorious, bringing all of us together.

Here, in Los Angeles, flags were waving and the responding voices grew louder, unlocking emotions usually held tightly inside.

Like a scene viewed through a wide-angle lens, the song took over, its volume increasing in a steady crescendo. Then I was completing the final words. As they pounded down in a majestically deliberate beat, the patriotic strength of America reverberated through the night, celebrating a landmark victory in defense of freedom.

"And I'd gladly stand up next to you and defend her still today,
'Cause there ain't no doubt I love this land—
God bless the U.S.A."

Lee Greenwood

Living in a Moment

Out on the road we have the wonderful opportunity, especially in the autograph lines, to sit and talk to everybody and get feedback on songs like my song, "Living in a Moment You Would Die For."

As an artist, it tells me we are doing our job when we're touching people's hearts. That's the whole purpose of music. It's what it's all about when we can make just a little difference in people's lives.

I had this seven-year-old boy and his father come up to me. The boy stuck his hand out and said, "Mr. Ty, I really love your song, 'Living in a Moment You Would Die For.'" And I said, "Well, that's great, son."

And as he turned to walk away, his father looked over and said, "No, he's really got a story to tell you. He lost his mom. She died during childbirth." And the boy turned and said, "To me, she was that person—she died for me. *I am living in the moment that she died for.*"

Ty Herndon

Ballerina on a Pink Horse

When I was a teenager, my sister Josie had an accident. At that time, she owned a beautiful music box topped with delicate figures of fine porcelain—a ballerina on a pink horse. The ballerina, pirouetting gracefully on one leg, balanced with one pointed toe secured firmly to the back of her steed. When the music played, both figures revolved with poise and elegance. The music box ballerina danced in the morning; she danced in the evening; she even danced in Josie's dreams. And whenever the ballerina danced, Josie's heart took wing.

When Mom presented that music box to Josie on her seventh birthday, my sister fell in love. She fell in love with dancing. She wanted to be that ballerina on a pink horse. Josie begged and pleaded with Mom for lessons. And our mother—never one to deny her daughters anything—said yes. To my great surprise, Josie approached ballet with a focus and a fervor that could only be described as true love.

While other kids were out playing, Josie was in dance class. And when she came home from school, she would go to her room, wind up the music box and dance some more. Sometimes her girlfriend, Anna, would come over.

Anna would help Josie with her regular school exercises and lessons, making sure my sister didn't stop until she got everything right. And when Josie was feeling down, Anna was there to offer encouragement and kind words. They were the best of friends.

Anna was always a nervous observer on those occasions when Josie chose to practice her balancing act on the high rail fence near our house. The height of the fence seemed to increase Josie's excitement, and the narrow width of the rails provided a welcome challenge to the limber, self-confident athlete. One day, several of Josie's schoolmates were also on hand to watch the high-altitude performance. Eager to demonstrate her skill as the kids egged her on, Josie attempted some of her most difficult maneuvers—including one where she placed the arch of her left foot just above the knee of her right leg while pirouetting. But she wasn't wearing her toe shoes at the time. And she wasn't performing in the safety of her bedroom or the practice hall. She lost her balance, tumbled to the ground, twisted her knee and was unable to get up. Soon afterward, Josie made the trip to our community hospital by ambulance with our mother at her side.

Now, Josie was lying on a hospital bed in traction with a cast around her leg. Today, the doctor was coming in to tell her when the cast was coming off. My sister was impatient; she wanted to be in her toe shoes and back on the dance floor.

Josie shivered with excitement when the doctor finally entered the room. But he had bad news. The X rays confirmed that her leg would heal fairly well, but she could never dance again. He said her knee could not take the pressure, nor would it support the agility needed for ballet.

Josie was stunned. She stared at the doctor in disbelief. His news had wounded her more than the fall. With the thought of never dancing again, her heart fluttered to the ground like a wounded bird.

The first night home from the hospital was spent in a deep sleep. But morning brought no relief. The first thing Josie saw when she awoke was the music box. She picked up the fragile porcelain and threw it against the wall—hard. It shattered into a thousand pieces. For the first time since the doctor had spoken to her, my sister cried.

Josie stayed in her room for the next few weeks. Inconsolable, she wanted no sympathy or help from anyone. When Anna came to visit, Mom had to turn her away. For the rest of the summer, friends phoned and sent get-well cards. The calls went unanswered, and the cards were left unopened on Josie's dresser.

Finally, September came and it was time for school. Josie would have to leave the sanctuary of her room. Now, even though the cast was gone and she wore a temporary knee brace, Josie was still on crutches.

Mom bought her a new dress in the hope of cheering her up, but to no avail. Josie felt lost and abandoned. Without her dream, there was no joy in her heart. So, with her backpack slung over her shoulder, Josie grabbed her crutches and left the house. Mom and I watched as she walked toward the school bus. Anna was there, waiting on the corner.

Josie had turned Anna away during that long summer, but now there was a strange attraction. You see, Anna had worn leg braces and used crutches most of her life. The polio virus had crippled her when she was only five. Anna had always dreamed of becoming a runner and competing in the Olympics. But as her disability grew worse and there proved to be no cause for hope, Anna was still a happy person. Deep in her heart, Anna knew she was a runner. She always had been and always would be.

As the two girls drew closer, they both started to cry. Then they began laughing—right out loud! They laughed until they cried. And for the first time since the accident, Josie smiled. Like Anna and her dreams of running, Josie knew she could never dance again. But deep inside, my sister would always be a ballerina on a pink horse. She always was and always will be. With that thought, her heart took wing and soared.

Barry Ettenger

6

THE POWER OF A SONG

*Music has a way of reaching into the
hidden corners of the mind and heart
and stirring a soul.*

Reverend Robert Schuller

Achy Breaky Heart

Don Von Tress wrote "Achy Breaky Heart" in early 1990. At that time, Don was hanging wallpaper for a living. He began the song while driving around in his van from one job site to another. As Don tells it . . .

> *I spent about 80 percent of my time on the road driving between jobs. Most of that time was spent writing. I remember singing the chorus of "Achy Breaky Heart" into a little tape recorder and thinking I had something pretty good. When I got home that night, I pulled out my new guitar and amplifier I had gotten for Christmas of 1989. The new guitar had really inspired my writing, something I had been pursuing since 1963 with little success, and the signature guitar riff on the song came pretty quickly. When I finished the song that night, some people may think this is crazy, but I distinctly remember having a clear vision of little kids singing and dancing. It was overwhelming and I felt then that "Achy Breaky Heart" was going to be special.*

It was ravaged by the critics. Travis Tritt said aloud what many other country artists were whispering under their breath—that this song did not represent country music, nor did Billy Ray Cyrus have any right to call himself a country artist.

But Billy Ray's fans didn't care what the critics, or Travis, said. They turned out in droves at his concerts and at the record stores. The *Some Gave All* album soared past platinum sales of 1 million and continues selling today with a total sales figure of close to 10 million.

In the letters we received from Billy Ray Cyrus's fans, they spoke of how "Achy Breaky Heart" had miraculously helped cure physical ailments, end lonely bouts of depression and even served as the impetus for one woman's one hundred–pound weight loss. Many people wrote that they had never been country music fans until they heard Billy Ray and were converted by his rock-tinged, "twang-less" vocals. Scores of young people from toddlers to teenagers, traditionally not a prime listening audience for country music, were infected by the "Cyrus Virus."

One of these new young fans was eleven-year-old Brooke Gall of Susquehanna, Pennsylvania.

Brooke hung Billy Ray posters all over her bedroom, where she spent hours listening to his music. She wore Billy Ray T-shirts and watched CMT (Country Music Television), eagerly awaiting each time they would air a Billy Ray video.

Brooke Gall was like millions of other preteen girls—a Billy Ray fanatic. But unlike most of the other young girls, Brooke was different. She was indeed a special fan—for Brooke has Down's syndrome.

One of the more serious characteristics of Down's syndrome can be heart defects. Brooke had her first heart surgery at sixteen months of age when doctors repaired a hole between the chambers of her heart.

Her second heart surgery took place on September 24, 1992, just three months after her eleventh birthday.

Brooke had contracted a virus which attacks the heart. The virus caused scar tissue to form on the walls of her heart valve. Surgery was scheduled to repair the valve, or, if necessary, replace it. The doctors decided the valve had to be replaced. The procedure would be risky, with Brooke facing a fifty-fifty chance of surviving.

Brooke traveled to University Hospital in Syracuse, New York, ninety miles from her home in Susquehanna. Her mom and stepdad, Mr. and Mrs. Scott Cooper, checked into the Ronald McDonald house near the hospital so they could be by Brooke's side for support.

The day Brooke was admitted to the hospital, she wore her favorite outfit. Not a lacy dress, or a fancy skirt and blouse, but her prized possession—a Billy Ray Cyrus "Achy Breaky" T-shirt.

Her family anxiously awaited as the surgery began. Hours later, the operation was successfully completed. Brooke was placed on a respirator and given morphine. Now her family began perhaps the most difficult wait— to see if Brooke's young body could survive the stress of the operation.

Brooke was unresponsive the first day after the surgery. The second day came and went. Brooke remained on the respirator unresponsive. On the third day, still no signs of consciousness. Late on the fourth day following the surgery, the doctors grew increasingly concerned about Brooke's failure to respond. They discussed doing a tracheotomy, another surgical procedure that would tax Brooke's already fragile body. The doctors finally asked the family if they could think of something—anything— that the family could bring in that Brooke might possibly respond to. Brooke's family had exactly what the doctor ordered. The *Some Gave All* cassette by Billy Ray Cyrus.

On the fifth day, as Brooke was on the downside of her dose of paralyzer, her family watched as they started the cassette on "Achy Breaky Heart." After not moving for five days, Brooke literally, in seconds, began to sway her arms in a dancing motion while still in her hospital bed on the respirator. Within an hour, Brooke was off the respirator, sitting up in the bed and asking for some of Ronald McDonald's French fries.

At 4:00 A.M. the following morning, Brooke was still wide awake and had all the nurses in the cardiac care unit enthusiastically "boogyin'" with her to Billy Ray's music.

A short time later, Brooke had recuperated enough from her surgery to leave the hospital. As she was walking out of the hospital, she was wearing yet another special T-shirt, one her family had custom-made for her during her hospital stay. The words they had imprinted on the shirt said what Brooke's smile reflected—MY ACHY BREAKY HEART IS ALL BETTER NOW.

Once Brooke had fully recuperated from her operation, she had one thing on her mind—meeting Billy Ray Cyrus in person. Brooke's grandmother wrote Billy Ray's manager, Jack McFadden, and told him the story of Brooke's miraculous recovery. Billy Ray was to be in Binghamton, New York, on November 3, for a concert. Arrangements were made for Brooke and her family to attend the show and meet Billy Ray backstage.

Their tickets were three rows from the stage, but evidently Billy Ray knew where his biggest fan was sitting that night. Brooke's mom says Billy Ray spent 90 percent of the concert right in front of Brooke. He even tossed one of his coveted towels, used to wipe his brow, directly to Brooke.

Afterward, the entire family went backstage. Brooke was beyond thrilled at meeting her idol, but she was not shy. She asked to sing "Achy Breaky Heart" together with Billy Ray. There possibly has never been a more touching duet. Brooke then presented Billy Ray with a rose she had brought to the concert. Billy Ray seemed genuinely moved. He proved it by asking, "Brooke, do you like flowers?" When Brooke replied, "Yes," Billy Ray scooped up every rose he had been given that night by hundreds of fans and gave them all to Brooke.

As Brooke left the arena that night, she was smiling just as she had been when she left the hospital a year earlier. She was once again wearing a T-shirt. A picture of Billy Ray Cyrus was on the front, and on the back was the title of her favorite song—"Achy Breaky Heart." A simple, childlike song which had touched millions, but perhaps saved the life of one—Brooke Gall.

Bruce Burch

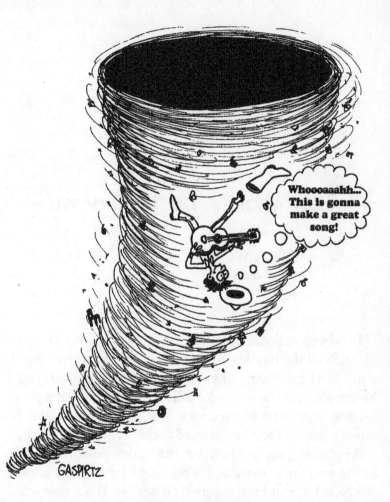

When life hands you a lemon,
make lemonade.

Just What the Doctor Ordered

God respects you when you work, but he loves you when you sing.

Cliffie Stone

I've been asked a million times why I've chosen to put up with all the hassles and inconveniences of working the road all these years when I could have easily stayed in Nashville, written songs for a living, and enjoyed a peaceful and comfortable existence. My reply is now and has always been: Nobody applauds when you write a song.

Applause surely must be the most powerful aphrodisiac known to mankind. The quest for it is a disease of the blood. Or, at best, a genetic disorder. What else would cause an apparently rational person of sound body and mind to pack his belongings and heedlessly ride away from his spouse and family in order to pursue such a nomadic and pointless existence? I mean, it's not like entertainers cure cancer or anything.

Or do we?

I once rode all night and half a day through a blinding snowstorm only to arrive in the little North Dakota town where we were booked to perform to find our concert had been canceled because of the weather. A handful of people hadn't heard the news, however, and had managed somehow to brave the elements and make their way to the auditorium.

Normally, under such circumstances, no one would expect the entertainers to perform. All performance contracts contain an "Act of God" clause stating that if something out of human control occurs, the contract becomes null and void.

The promoter was under no obligation to pay us for the date. Likewise, we had no obligation to go on stage. We were cold, tired and hungry. The endless miles on a narrow, snow-swept highway had taken their toll. But there was something in the eyes of those few fans who had shown up that told us how badly they wanted to hear the music they knew we could play if only we would.

A small kitchen was off to the side of the auditorium, and the promoter offered to cook us some food. We warmed our hands by the steaming heat rising off a small group of antiquated radiator coils in the corner of the hallway and talked the situation over. There was certainly no place else for us to go. The entire town was held prisoner by the storm. Why not drink some coffee, fill our bellies and pick a little country music?

Which is exactly what we did. I told the audience they'd better treat us real good, though, because we had 'em outnumbered. We gave them our time and our talents and, in return, they were more than generous to us with their applause.

When our show was over, we stood around for a while and signed a few autographs and visited with the people. An elderly lady, wearing a heavy coat that had obviously kept her warm for many long winters, her head wrapped in a faded blue scarf, approached the stage where I was standing.

"You don't know how much this evening has meant to me," she said, reaching up for my hand and looking deeply into my eyes.

"Well, we've enjoyed it, too," I replied, smiling and giving her hand a slight squeeze.

"My husband just passed away," she said sadly, lowering her head. "I haven't been out of the house since he died except to go to the grocery store and to church. I didn't really want to come here today, but my daughter insisted on bringing me. My husband and I had lots of your records, and we used to enjoy so much watching you on TV."

I smiled and thanked her.

"I'm so glad to get to meet you," she continued. "Thank you for playing and singing for such a small crowd. Today is the first time I've smiled since my husband died. Your music has helped me to forget my problems for a while."

Okay, so entertainers don't cure cancer. But maybe, every once in a while, we cure some other things that are almost as important.

Whisperin' Bill Anderson

It's Not the End of the World

If you find it in your heart to care for somebody else, you will have succeeded.

Maya Angelou

I'll never forget one cold night in Michigan while I was on tour with Alan Jackson. A security man handed me a note passed along from a lady in the audience:

> *I am here tonight to hear one song, "It's Not the End of the World." My son bought two tickets for this show, and he loved this song. He also bought these tickets a long way ahead of time before we knew he was sick with advanced cancer. He passed away last month after a very short illness. This song made him happy until the end, and that made me very, very happy. Tonight, I sit here alone with an extra ticket—so please make us happy and play our song.*

Before I received this note I was so pumped up and excited for the show. But the note just floored me. I gave the note to my manager and asked him to arrange for the lady to come backstage to my preshow meet-and-greet area. Soon, I spotted her walking up the hall toward me. She was so happy, her face was lit up with a thousand-watt smile. It was wonderful! I sang the song to her before I went on. The lady was so happy, and I thought perhaps I understood what she was feeling. In her heart, she knew her son was living a better life and that made me feel good in my heart.

Because of the emotion of that song, none of us will ever be the same again. I believe that song completely changed three lives that night. To the boy who had left and was looking down at us, it helped him find his way to the next life. To the mother, it allowed her to feel a certain acceptance and gladness for his leaving and eased the pain of her loss. And it taught me that it's okay to be excited and high about being an entertainer privileged to bring happiness and gladness into people's lives. It also taught me never to forget to keep my feet on the ground. . . . and to always remember the things that come from the heart.

Emilio

I Will Always Love You

Your talent is God's gift to you. How you use it is your gift to God.

Country Saying

Some time ago I was in an airport in Somewhere, U.S.A., when a lovely, well-dressed lady came up to me and said, "I hope I'm not intruding on your privacy, but I could not let this moment go by, as I feel that it was God's will that I see you today. I want to thank you, on behalf of my family, for writing, 'I Will Always Love You.'

"When my father, a very proud and quiet man, was dying of cancer a few months ago, he found it very difficult to tell his family how he felt and what he was thinking. So, he asked our mother to bring his tape of 'I Will Always Love You' to the hospital. Each time we kids would come over, he would play it.

> *If I should stay*
> *I would only be in your way.*
> *So I'll go,*
> *But I know*

I'll think of you each step of the way.
And I will always love you,
I will always love you.

"The words seemed to be perfect for what he wanted to say, not only to us kids but to Mother as well."

Bitter-sweet memories,
That is all I am taking with me.
Good-bye. Please don't you cry,
'Cause we both know I'm not what you need.
But I will always love you.

"We also played the tape, your version, at the funeral."

I hope life treats you kind,
And I hope you have all you dream of.
I wish you joy and happiness;
But above all this, I wish you love.

"So God bless you, Dolly Parton."

And I will always love you, I will always love you.
Yes, I will always love you, I will always love you.

Everyone standing around, including myself, was crying like children at such a sweet and sad story. I hugged her and thanked her also for touching my life.

When I got to the plane, I bowed my head and thanked God for giving me the talent to touch people with my gift.

Dolly Parton

Healing Music

On May 8, 1994, our sixteen-year-old son, Joshua, died. At first, my wife, Marlis, and I thought he had the flu, but when he didn't improve after a few days, we took him to our local hospital. The following morning, Josh was taken by medevac helicopter to a larger hospital. . . . but he died anyway. The doctors think he had Rocky Mountain spotted fever, but the tests were not conclusive.

I wasn't with Josh when he died. He asked for me very late that night—after he was airlifted—but I had a fractured ankle and couldn't endure standing on it for hours at a time. Instead, my daughter, Sarah, and I had planned to make the trip early the following morning. My wife and her mother were at the hospital with Joshua. That night, while I was on the telephone with my wife, the doctor brought her the news—that our Josh was in a bad way and the process that was killing him couldn't be stopped.

I demanded to have the phone put up to Joshua's ear and held there. Then I said my good-byes and told him how much I loved him and how proud I was to be his father. Afterward, my wife and I stayed together by telephone for his last moments—and cried and cried. I wasn't there for my son, to hold his hand as he went into eternity with our Lord. That haunts me, to this day, every day.

I spoke a few words at the funeral for my son. I just had to. Sarah placed a rose on her brother's casket, I climbed to the pulpit using my cane. I think the most important thing I said was, "Joshua looked one more time into his mother's face, closed his eyes in death and smiled. He looked into the face of the person who had brought him into the world. And as he died, he smiled, because he saw Jesus, the face of the One who was taking him into his eternal world, and eternal life."

Joshua wanted to live in the mountains after college. So, we had his remains cremated and took them to the south-west corner of Colorado. Seven miles up an old mining road, at an elevation of ten thousand feet with a jagged mountain range in the background, we found a hidden meadow. There, we placed a marking stone level into the ground. It reads "Josh Moodie, Beloved Son and Brother, 1977-1994." We scattered his ashes there.

The following week, my kinfolk who live in the area and found the spot for us, took some other family members to "Joshua's Meadow." They discovered that a herd of wild horses had spent the night. Not only did Josh love horses, his middle name, Philip, means "lover of horses."

Up until Josh's death, ours had been a very musical family. Josh played the French horn for seven years and was in his high school's marching band. Sarah is gifted with a wonderful voice and won singing contests in middle school. Both children took private lessons. Our family has an extremely large collection of CDs—gospel and, especially, Christmas music. Music was always in our home, in our car and in our lives.

But when Josh died, music died for my family. The stereo was idle—as was the car radio, tape deck and portable stereo. Christmas songs were nothing but background music for our heartache. Sarah's voice lessons went by without practice and continued only with parental insistence. Her singing was without life—flat, expressionless, totally lacking in joy.

My sadness knew no bounds. Even breathing caused sharp pain—the grief was just too much for me. Too much! I thought to myself, *God must have made a mistake here, when he took my Josh.*

I was afraid I had to end my pain the only way I knew how—with a pistol. I knew I couldn't live with the pain—not even for my family and friends!

Then something incredible happened! I heard Kathy Mattea sing "Mary, Did You Know?" on a 1994 Christmas show on TV. I had never heard of this country music star, but pieces of that song remained with me for all of 1995. When the Christmas season came again, I found out who Kathy Mattea was and bought her CD, *Good News*.

The first time I played it for my family, our whole house seemed to change—to brighten. Just as the radiance of spring follows the gloom of a long winter, music came alive in our home once more. We played that CD over and over, and it made us feel *wonderful.* Our collection of other Christmas CDs once again gave us the joy we had known from them when Josh was alive. We began singing with the music, just like before. What a gift *Good News* was to us. When I cleaned out Joshua's room—three years after his death—it took me a week. I would work awhile, then go hide in my room and cry and sob for a while. Then back and forth. But I had Kathy singing to me the entire time. It was as if she was in the room with me, talking and encouraging and loving me through her music.

Last year, I went to a Kathy Mattea concert in Tulsa and as a fan club member, I was allowed to meet her. When I told her my name, she said, "You're the 'Walter' who sent me the letter about your son, aren't you?" Then she gave me what I believe is the biggest hug I've ever had. She felt the pain and suffering and loss that I did, and she loved me up the best she could as a friend! Then, knowing that I was very intimidated by her status in the music world, she stood next to me, held my hand and talked for what seemed like forever while pictures were taken of us together.

During the Christmas service at our church last year, Sarah sang Kathy's song "Mary, Did You Know" as a solo, accompanied only by her music teacher on the guitar. My wife and I were transported as we listened to the very song that healed me—and our family—and gave us back living in this world, not just hanging on.

Walter Moodie

More Chicken Soup?

Everyone has a song in him.

Cliffie Stone

Just as "everyone has a song in him," we believe everyone has a story in him or her. Many of the stories and poems you have read in this book were submitted by readers like yourself who had read earlier *Chicken Soup for the Soul* books. We are planning to publish six to eight new *Chicken Soup for the Soul* books every year, and we invite you to contribute a story to one of these future volumes.

Stories may be up to 1,200 words and must uplift, comfort, encourage or inspire. You may submit an original piece or something you clip out of a local newspaper, a magazine, a church bulletin or a company newsletter. It might be something you receive by fax, your favorite quotation or a personal experience that has touched you deeply.

In addition to future servings of *Chicken Soup for the Soul*, some of the other books we have planned are *Chicken Soup for the Teenage Soul II*, and *A Second Chicken Soup for the . . . Country Soul, Kid's Soul, Woman's Soul, Christian Soul* and *Pet Lover's Soul*, as well as the following new books: *Chicken Soup for the . . . Parent's Soul, Teacher's Soul, Single Soul, Laughing Soul, Grieving Soul, Divorced Soul* and *Sports Fan's Soul.*

Just send a copy of your stories and other pieces, indicating which edition they are for, to the following address:

Chicken Soup for the *(Specify Which Edition)* Soul
P.O. Box 30880 • Santa Barbara, CA 93130
phone: 805-563-2935 • fax: 805-563-2945
To send e-mail or to visit our Web site:
www.chickensoup.com

We will be sure that both you and the author are credited for your submission.

Soup Kitchens for the Soul

One of the most exciting developments with *Chicken Soup for the Soul* was the impact it had on readers who are welfare recipients, homeless, at-risk students or those incarcerated in local jails and state prisons.

As a result, we established the Soup Kitchens for the Soul Project, which donates *Chicken Soup for the Soul* books to individuals and social service organizations that cannot afford to purchase them.

We have already donated over twenty-five thousand copies of *Chicken Soup for the Soul* books to men and women in prisons, halfway houses, homeless shelters, battered women's shelters, literacy programs, inner-city schools, AIDS hospices, hospitals, churches, and other organizations that serve adults and teenagers in need.

Many of these books are provided by the publisher and the authors, but an equal number have been donated by readers like yourself. We welcome and invite your participation in this project in the following ways. For every $15.95 you contribute, we will send two copies of *Chicken Soup for the Country Soul* to programs that support people in need. We also invite you to submit the names of worthy programs that you think should receive copies of the books.

The program is administered by the Foundation for Self-Esteem in Culver City, California. Please make your check payable to The Foundation for Self-Esteem and send it to:

Soup Kitchens for the Soul
The Foundation for Self-Esteem
6035 Bristol Parkway • Culver City, CA 90230
or call 310-568-1505 and make your contribution
by credit card

We will acknowledge receipt of your contribution and let you know where the books you paid for were sent.

Opry Trust Fund

In the spirit of supporting all people involved in the country music industry, we have selected the Opry Trust Fund to receive a portion of the profits generated from the paperback sales of *Chicken Soup for the Country Soul.*

The Opry Trust Fund was created in 1965 to give financial assistance in time of need, emergency or catastrophe to those employed in the country music industry or their families. They need not be associated with the Grand Ole Opry to receive benefits.

Gaylord Entertainment Company underwrites all administrative expenses for the Opry Trust Fund, and no salaries are charged to the fund. The trust fund board approves all grants.

The financial gifts have been used for various emergencies, from assuring medicine and food, to paying hospital and funeral expenses.

The Opry Trust Fund exemplifies the country music industry, helping its own less fortunate to overcome financial and emotional crisis.

If you would like to help support the Opry Trust Fund, you can send a tax-deductible contribution to:

The Opry Trust Fund
2804 Opryland Drive
Nashville, TN 37214
phone: 615-889-7502

Trees Around the World, Inc.

The *Chicken Soup for the Soul* organization is committed to ensuring that as many trees as possible are planted to nourish the environment and nourish humanity.

Trees help combat pollution by trapping smog from auto and industrial emissions. In fact, one tree absorbs as much as forty-eight pounds of carbon dioxide per year. Trees play a key role in combating the greenhouse effect, thereby reducing the threat of global warming. Trees beautify urban areas, conserve water, prevent storm water pollution, provide food and habitat for wildlife, and increase property values by as much as 15 percent.

A portion of the proceeds from *A 4th Course of Chicken Soup for the Soul* enabled the National Arbor Day Foundation to plant 200,000 trees! *Chicken Soup for the Country Soul* will also donate a generous portion of their proceeds to Trees Around the World, Inc.

In addition, we invite you to plant three trees: One for the day you were born; one for when you die; and the other for the first time you fell in love.

Thank you for your participation in managing your piece of the ecosystem and instilling respect for Mother Earth.

Who Is Jack Canfield?

Jack Canfield is a bestselling author with over twenty-three books published, including nine *New York Times* bestsellers. He is also a dynamic and entertaining keynote speaker and a highly sought-after trainer.

Jack spent his childhood years growing up in Wheeling, West Virginia, where he fell in love with country music on local radio station WWVA and attended many a Saturday Night Jamboree, Wheeling's version of the Grand Ole Opry. Jack's love of country music led to his playing the guitar and singing in a popular local folksinging group at the time, the New American Travellers. Jack owns what he believes is one of the largest collections of country music around.

Jack is the author and narrator of several bestselling audio- and videocassette programs including *Self-Esteem and Peak Performance, How to Build High Self-Esteem* and *The STAR Program*. He is a regularly consulted expert for radio and television broadcasts, and has published a total of twenty-three books—all bestsellers within their categories—including seventeen *Chicken Soup for the Soul* books, *The Aladdin Factor, Heart at Work, One Hundred Ways to Build Self-Concept in the Classroom* and *Dare to Win*.

Jack conducts keynote speeches for about seventy-five groups each year. His clients have included schools and school districts in all fifty states, over one hundred education associations including the American School Counselors Association and Californians for a Drug Free Youth, plus corporate clients such as AT&T, Campbell Soup, Clairol, Domino's Pizza, GE, New England Telephone, Re/Max, Sunkist, Supercuts and Virgin Records.

Jack conducts an annual seven-day Training of Trainers Program in the areas of building self-esteem and achieving peak performance in all areas of your life. The program attracts educators, counselors, parenting trainers, corporate trainers, professional speakers, ministers, youth workers and others.

To contact Jack for further information about his books, tapes and trainings, or to schedule him for a keynote speech, please contact:

The Canfield Training Group
P.O. Box 30880 • Santa Barbara, CA 93130
phone: 805-563-2935 • fax: 805-563-2945
To send e-mail or to visit his Web site: www.chickensoup.com

Who Is Mark Victor Hansen?

Mark Victor Hansen is a professional speaker who, in more than two decades, has made over four thousand presentations to more than 2 million people in thirty-two countries. His presentations cover sales excellence and strategies; personal empowerment and development; and how to triple your income and double your time off.

Mark has spent a lifetime dedicated to his mission of making a profound and positive difference in people's lives. Throughout his career, he has inspired hundreds of thousands of people to create a more powerful and purposeful future for themselves while stimulating the sale of billions of dollars worth of goods and services.

Mark is a prolific writer and has authored *Future Diary, How to Achieve Total Prosperity* and *The Miracle of Tithing.* He is coauthor of the *Chicken Soup for the Soul* series, *Dare to Win* and *The Aladdin Factor* (all with Jack Canfield) and *The Master Motivator* (with Joe Batten).

Mark has also produced a complete library of personal empowerment audio- and videocassette programs that have enabled his listeners to recognize and use their innate abilities in their business and personal lives. His message has made him a popular television and radio personality, with appearances on ABC, NBC, CBS, HBO, PBS, CNN, Prime Time Country, Crook & Chase and TNN News. He has also appeared on the cover of numerous magazines, including *Success, Entrepreneur* and *Changes.*

Mark is a big man with a heart and spirit to match—an inspiration to all who seek to better themselves.

For further information about Mark contact:

P.O. Box 7665 • Newport Beach, CA 92658
phone: 714-759-9304 or 800-433-2314
fax: 714-722-6912
To send e-mail or to visit his Web site: www.chickensoup.com

Who Is Ron Camacho?

I started in rock and worked my way up to country.

Conway Twitty

Ron Camacho grew up in a small rural town in the Mohawk River valley of upstate New York. Raised by his mother, he and his brother learned respect for the country life.

Ron attended the State University of Buffalo as an art major. While at Buffalo he started the "fanzine" known as the *Shakin' Street Gazette* and began his career as a music critic. Within two years he was responsible for getting a band signed to Columbia records, and left college to become a road manager. The following year, he began work with the band Blood, Sweat and Tears.

For the next twenty years Ron road managed, managed, promoted or bodyguarded some of the top performers in pop and rock music.

Over this time Ron has organized, cosponsored or worked with charities for his favorite organizations supporting children. He has been involved with benefit concerts for Find the Children, Feed the Children, Unite for Pediatric AIDS and the T. J. Martell Foundation, to name a few.

After leaving rock 'n' roll Ron became involved with the California Country Music Association, leading the stars onto the Pomona fairgrounds at the first Fan Fests. Ron became hooked on country music and pursued it with the same enthusiasm that he had for rock.

With his three-year journey completed, he has set up his company, American Entertainment Concepts, in Nashville, Tennessee. This promotion production team will promote *Chicken Soup for the Country Soul* around the world, proudly bringing country music and lifestyle with it.

To contact Ron for events surrounding the book promotion, media appearances and concerts, please contact:

American Entertainment Concepts
c/o Ron Camacho
73 White Bridge Rd., Ste. 103-238 • Nashville, TN 37205
phone: 615-353-0223 • fax: 615-353-8872
To send e-mail or to visit his Web site: www.amentco.com

Contributors

Several of the stories in this book were taken from previously published sources such as books, magazines and newspapers. Those sources are acknowledged in the permissions section. However, most of the stories in the book were submitted by country singers, songwriters and country fans like yourself who had read our previous *Chicken Soup for the Soul* books and who responded to our request for stories. We have included information about these authors and contributors below.

Bill Anderson is a nationally known television personality, star of the Grand Ole Opry and member of the Songwriters' Hall of Fame. He has released over fifty albums, written over one thousand songs, and authored two books. He can be reached at P.O. Box 888, Hermitage, TN 37076.

H. R. Ayers is a practicing attorney, with home and offices in Goodlettsville, Tennessee (a suburb of Nashville). He was born in Alderson, West Virginia, and is presently working on a book of stories, true and almost true, about his early life in the mountains of West Virginia during the forties and fifties. The book will be entitled *Tales from the End of the Bridge*.

Jonnie Barnett is a songwriter whose songs have been recorded by major artists in the blues, R&B, country, jazz and rock categories. He has acted in major motion pictures and television. In 1997 he was nominated for a W. C. Handy Award for Blues Song of the Year. He owes all his success to his beautiful wife Barbara. He can be reached at Broadmoor Music, 1007 McMahan Ave., Nashville, TN 37216.

Rita Batts is a housewife and mother, who lives in St. Catharines, Ontario, Canada. Rita and her husband, Greg, have been married for twenty-six years. They have been blessed with two daughters, Kelly, age twenty, and Carrie, age seventeen. "My family is my constant source of strength and inspiration."

Paul Brandt is a Reprise Records recording artist. His debut album *Calm Before the Storm* has sold in excess of 1 million copies in North America. His second release is entitled *Outside the Frame*. Paul is best known for his hits "I Do," "My Heart Has a History," "What's Come Over You" and "I Meant to Do That." Paul can be reached at Paul Brandt Fan Club, P.O. Box 57144, Sunridge Postal Outlet, Calgary, Alberta, Canada, T1Y 5TO, or at *pbfanclb@cadvision.com*.

Kippi Brannon was signed to MCA Records at the age of fifteen. As one of the youngest signees, she had two Top 40 hits and was nominated in 1982 for Top New Female Vocalist Award by the Academy of Country Music. She toured with such acts as George Strait, Alabama, Bob Hope, and others until making the decision to lead a more normal life and pursue a college education. However, in 1997, she returned to the music industry with "Daddy's Little Girl," which was a Top 40 hit.

Bruce Burch is a songwriter with two number-one songs to his credit, "Rumor Has It," and "It's Your Call," both recorded by Reba McEntire. He is also the author of *Songs That Changed Our Lives,* inspirational stories of how music has touched people's lives. Bruce can be reached at 119 Bowling Ave., Nashville, TN 37205.

Monty Byrom is one of six members of the band BIG HOUSE. Monty is the lead singer and guitarist; David Neuhauser and Chuck Seaton on guitar; Sonny California on harmonica and percussion; Ron Mitchell on Bass and Tanner Byrom on drums. The band hails from Bakersfield, California. BIG HOUSE's sparse productions, including their first release, "Cold Outside," leaves the listener moved, but still feeding good. The BIG HOUSE name? David explains, "If all of our musical influences came to spend the night, we would need one."

Jean M. Calvert is John Berry's Fan Club manager. For membership information, please write to John Berry's Fan Club, The Pack, 1807 N. Dixie Ave., #116, Elizabethtown, KY 42701.

Martha Campbell is a graduate of Washington University St. Louis School of Fine Arts, and a former writer/designer for Hallmark Cards. She has been a freelance cartoonist and book illustrator since 1973. She can be reached at P.O. Box 2538, Harrison, AR, 72602 , or *marthaf@alltel.net* or by calling 870-741-5323.

Dave Carpenter has been a full-time cartoonist and humorous illustrator since 1981. His cartoons have appeared in *Barron's,* the *Wall Street Journal, Forbes, Better Homes & Gardens, Good Housekeeping, Woman's World, First, The Saturday Evening Post* and numerous other publications. Dave can be reached at P.O. Box 520, Emmetsburg, IA 50536, or by calling 712-852-3725.

Gary Chapman is the multi-talented host of *PrimeTime Country,* seen nightly by millions of people on The Nashville Network (TNN). In addition, Gary is an award-winning singer/songwriter with seven records to his credit, including his most recent recording, *The Gift.* He resides in Nashville, Tennessee, with his wife, Amy Grant, and three children. He can be reached c/o Friends of Gary, P.O. Box 3627, Brentwood, TN 37024-3627.

Dan Clark is the international ambassador of the "Art of Being Alive." He has spoken to over 2 million people worldwide. Dan is an actor, songwriter, recording artist, video producer and award-winning athlete. He is the well-known author of seven books, including *Getting High—How to Really Do It, One Minute Messages, The Art of Being Alive* and *Puppies for Sale and Other Inspirational Tales.* He can be reached at P.O. Box 8689, Salt Lake City, UT 84108, or by calling 801-485-5755.

Robert Crum, a writer and photographer, lives in Corvallis, Oregon. He has written and photographed two children's books with Simon & Schuster: *Let's Rodeo,* about kids who compete in rodeos, and *Eagle Drum,* on Native American powwows. He has also written articles for such magazines as *Sierra, Wildlife Conservation* and *Harvard Magazine.*

Joe Diffie is a Sony recording artist who has sold 5 million albums in the country music field over the last seven years. Known for his soulful and distinctive vocals, he has had numerous chart-topping singles, 25 million radio spins, and was named the 1997 Humanitarian of the Year for his extensive charity work.

Robert J. (Jack) Duncan is a freelance writer whose work has been published in *Reader's Digest* and elsewhere. A believer in lifelong learning, he recently earned a second master's degree. He is a former president of the Texas Folklore Society. His manuscript on Southwestern artist/illustrator Ben Carlton Mead has been accepted for publication by the University of North Texas Press. He works as an employment/training specialist for Goodwill Industries. Jack is married to his McKinney (Texas) high school sweetheart, Elizabeth. They have two grown sons and three small grandsons. Their Duncan Enterprises is a mail-order book business specializing in rare Southwestern history and folklore. Duncan can be reached at 1801 Erwin Place, McKinney, TX 75069, or *je_duncan@rocketmail.com.*

Barry Ettenger is a writer/photographer with over ten years of experience in the entertainment industry. His current projects include screenplays and children's books. Originally from the Northeast, he now resides in Nashville, Tennesse. Barry can be reached at 615-383-0075.

Kathy Fasig is a public school teacher in Nashville, Tennessee. She has taught kindergarten and first grade since 1976. She has a bachelor's and master's degree in elementary education. She and her husband, Trice, have two children, Amy and Jacob. "Grandfather's Clock" was written in the memory of her grandfather, Roy Wooten.

Fred Foster is the founder of Monument Records and The Combine Music Group. He discovered and/or produced such artists as Roy Orbison, Dolly Parton, Willie Nelson, Boots Randolph, Ray Stevens, The Gatlins, Kris Kristofferson, Grandpa Jones, Charlie McCoy, plus many others. Fred has produced 136 Top 20 records in all fields of music; many were number one, most were Top 10. Fred can be reached at 1103-B 17th Ave. South, Nashville, TN 37212, or by calling 615-327-0031.

Victor Fried's unique artistry combines storytelling with poetry demonstrating inspirational truths that have moved audiences across the nation. If you are interested in having Victor come speak to your church or civic organization, write to The Dreamwaver Project, 9 Music Square South, Ste. 181, Nashville, TN 37203, or call 615-331-6758.

Carla M. Fulcher co-owns E.S.P. Corporation, an entertainment labor provider for the music industry headquartered in Nashville, Tennessee. Though poetry, compositions and technical writings are her specialties, she will soon begin the third volume of a trilogy of light-hearted and warm short stories from childhood for possible future publication. Carla can be reached c/o E.S.P. Corporation, 301 Preakness Dr., Antioch, TN 37013.

Oliver Gaspirtz is an award-winning cartoonist. His work has been exhibited at numerous cartoon art museums around the world. His cartoons have appeared in countless magazines and in over a dozen books. His latest book, *A Treasury of Police Humor,* is available at Barnes & Noble, or directly from the publisher at Lincoln-Herndon Press, 818 South Dirksen Parkway, Springfield, IL 62703, or by calling 217-522-2732.

Merilyn Morris Gilliam is the vice president of the Cheatham Co. Right to Life. "The love for children and their future inspire me, not only my own, but my families, friends and even those children I have never met." Merilyn can be reached at P.O. Box 141, Ashland City, TN 37015.

T. J. Greaney publishes a country lifestyle publication called *Country Line Magazine,* in central Texas. He is also an avid outdoorsman and outdoor writer. He is married with three children. He can be reached at P.O. Box 17245, Austin, TX 78760, or by calling 512-292-1113. His Web site is www.Country Linemagazine.com. You can send him e-mail at *CountryLine@juno.com.*

Lewis Grizzard was a nationally syndicated newspaper columnist and author of numerous books. He died in 1994. *The Grizzard Sampler,* a collection of his work, can be ordered by contacting Peachtree Publishers at 800-241-0113.

Jonny Hawkins is a long-time freelance cartoonist whose work has been seen in over two hundred publications, including *Barron's, Boy's Life, Air and Space* and many others. His services and his latest book, *Healing Humor,* are available by writing him at P.O. Box 188, Sherwood, MI 49089. He can be contacted by phone or fax at 517-741-3668.

Ty Herndon is an Epic Records recording artist. His first album, *Living in a Moment,* explored the depth of an artist who's been nominated for or won just about every Best New Male Award of the last year. Born in Meridian, Mississippi, and raised in Butler, Alabama, he was bit by the music bug in his youth. At an early age, he headed out for Nashville to try and make it. Sidelined by bad business dealings, he set out to do the honky-tonks-and-ice-houses circuit of Texas where he finished his musical education and graduated with honors by winning the Texas Entertainer of the Year in 1993. His new album, *Big Hopes,* was just released in May.

Becky Hobbs has written songs for Alabama, Conway Twitty, George Jones, Loretta Lynn, Glen Campbell, Emmylou Harris, Helen Reddy, Shirley Bassey and others. As an artist, she's recorded eighteen chart singles, six albums and has performed in over thirty-five countries. She can be reached at P.O. Box 150272, Nashville, TN 37215.

Jan Howard is a long time Grand Ole Opry member. She and Bill Anderson were honored with Duet of the Year from the Country Music Association. Jan has received numerous awards including Top Female Artist and Most Promising Female Artist, along with several awards for her songwriting. Her singles, "Evil On Your Mind" and "My Son," were nominated for Grammy Awards. Jan has a saying by which she has tried to live: "This is *not* a rehearsal . . . this *is* the show, and there are *no* retakes . . . the time is *now*." Her highly successful autobiography, *Sunshine and Shadow,* published in 1987, is true. Jan lived and wrote every word herself. She deserves to be where she is today, and wears her success well.

John Jarrard's history as a Nashville songwriter dates back to 1982 and includes more than one hundred of his songs and eleven number one singles by such artists as George Strait, Pam Tillis, Tracy Lawrence, Collin Raye and Alabama. His work has appeared on records that have sold more than 60 million copies.

Floanne Kersh, known in her hometown as "Showanne," is creator/writer/ director of The Entertainers, a musical-comedy team of performing retirees. Floanne writes for several papers, special programs and events. Her favorites are comedy-skit writing and "poetry from the heart." She can be reached at 809 Pineview Dr., Hattiesburg, MS 39401.

Rory Lee is a staff songwriter for the legendary Harlan Howard. He has had many songs recorded, one of which, "Someone You Used To Know" is on Collin Raye's latest album. He is hailed as one of Music Row's best storytellers, and as a writer of songs of virtue. Rory is a single father of two daughters, Heidi and Hopie. He can be reached at 412 Erin Lane, Nashville, TN 37221, or by calling Harlan Howard Songs at 615-321-9098.

Merlin Littlefield began his music business career in 1967, after graduating from Texas Christian University with majors in radio-TV-film and sociology. His career spans from Capitol Records, RCA, Stax and Capricorn Records, to his own management and publishing companies. He moved to Nashville in 1974, where he held the position of associate director of ASCAP until 1994. While at ASCAP, he signed such writer/artists as Reba McEntire, George Strait and Lyle Lovett. He has produced the ASCAP Awards for fifteen years and is the recipient of the Gospel Music Association's Dove Award. He has served as a board member on numerous music industry associations and committees. Merlin is presently president and owner of Nakomis Publishing. He can be reached at P.O. Box 25166, Nashville, TN 37202.

Walter W. Meade started writing at the age of fourteen. His first story was published in *Colliers* magazine when he was twenty-two. He wrote short fiction for the *Saturday Evening Post, Gentlemen's Quarterly* and several others. He then turned to writing nonfiction for magazines such as *Cosmopolitan, Redbook* and the *Reader's Digest.* Later he took a position in the publishing world and became the managing editor of *Cosmopolitan* and then the managing editor of the *Reader's Digest* Book Club. His last position in publishing was president and editor in chief of Avon Books, a position he held for ten years. Today, Walter is retired and writing articles for *Reader's Digest* as well as many other magazines and periodicals. He can be reached at 4561 N.W. 67th Terr., Lauderhill, FL 33319.

Walter Moodie is a disabled Vietnam veteran. He is married to Marlis and has a daughter, Sarah, and son, Joshua, who is in heaven. He is a writer of narrative poetry stories, none of which are published for monetary gain. He writes for the pleasure it brings to others. His story about Kathy Mattea was for her, and the money is being donated to a charity of her choice (AIDS).

Emilio Navaira is a native Texan who records country Tex-Mex Music. He also has a foundation for Santa Rosa Children's Hospital in San Antonio, Texas. Emilio is also a winner of many Latin awards and Grammy nominations. He performs around the world. For more information on Emilio or his fan club call 210-923-7191, or write to 719 W. Vestal, San Antonio, TX 78221.

Luke Reed is a native Oklahoman who now makes his home in Dickson, Tennessee. He is married to Carol Chatham-Reed and they have two sons, Austin and Sawyer. Luke has been a working cowboy, agriculture teacher, and horticulturist. He now makes his living as a songwriter. George Strait, Randy Travis, Red Steagall, The Crickets, and others have recorded his work. In 1996, he received the Will Rogers Award from the Academy of Western Artists.

Susan Wells Pardue is the award-winning author of children's stories and fiction that celebrates Southern folklore. Susan teaches creative writing and she promotes her innovative ideas through workshops and motivational lectures. She may be reached by fax at 615-758-5645, or by calling 615-758-5606.

Dolly Parton, throughout her career that has spanned decades, has contributed countless treasures to the world of music and entertainment. In 1993, the Country Music Association honored Dolly with a special television tribute and its first ever Country Music Honors Awards for her accomplishments as a performer, songwriter, actress, recording artist and humanitarian. She is a four-time Grammy Award winner and has earned eight Country Music Awards. Dolly is the recipient of three Academy Of Country Music awards and three People's Choice awards.

Reverend Malcolm Patton is currently pastor of Gallatin First United Methodist Church. He has been serving churches since 1957. He is married to Barbara who is an English teacher and they have two sons, Christopher and Timothy, and a grandson, Blake. Reverend Patton enjoys jogging, weight lifting and collecting antiques. He is on the board of directors of Cumberland Mental Health and member of the Lions Club.

Michael Peterson is a Reprise Records recording artist. With his debut album, Michael Peterson, he is *Billboard*'s Most Played New Artist in 1997. He is nominated for Academy Country Music and TNN/Music City News

Awards and is the top-selling new male artist of 1997. "I can't remember one moment in my life when music wasn't my friend, my favorite source of entertainment, my comfort and my encouragement." He is an artist driven with desire to invite us all to laugh, dance and consider our own lives—often simultaneously.

Joe M. Pritchard has worked with troubled kids and families for twenty years. Now pursuing a lifelong dream of writing, his first book, *Stepfather's Anonymous Playbook*, was published in 1997. His second book, *Of Mustard Seed & Men*, is forthcoming. To order his book, call 615-847-2066, or write to P.O. Box 367, Old Hickory, TN 37138.

Roxane Russell is from Hammond, Louisiana and graduated from Texas Christian University with a BSA in radio, TV and film. She is currently a feature producer for TNN working on such shows as *Opry Backstage*. A country music fan and historian, she has been a country music radio disc jockey, as well as a television news anchor and talk show host.

Phil Thomas's philosophy on life is reflected in the verses he writes. He has recited stories like "Raymond," and the more humorous, "Colorado Cool Aid," from the ELKO, Nevada, poet gathering, the San Antonio Stock Show, to the Italian Street Fair in Nashville, Tennessee. Phil is currently working on a children's story album. He can be reached at Route 4, Box 197 B, Linden, TN 37096, or by calling 931-589-5788.

Randy Travis is a Grammy Award-winning country artist and the first country artist signed by Dreamworks SKG. Gentle humility, musical integrity and easy-going humor are a combination that makes Randy one of the most charismatic stars of his generation. He has sold more than 20 million records, placed twenty-five brilliant singles in the top ten and paved the way for Garth Brooks, Clint Black, Alan Jackson and the rest of his multi-platinum contemporaries.

Richard Tripp is the founder and director of Care of Poor People (COPP) Inc. He is a man who has one main dedicated goal—to get the homeless and hurting brothers and sisters off the streets of America and back into housing and employment. He is a self-made man taking on the system by coming up with original ideas for housing and employment training—ideas that he got from living it himself. He has published a book, *It's Hip to Help the Homeless: How to Give a Hand Up Instead of a Handout*. If you would like to support Richard and the work that he is doing or start you own organization, please contact him at 816-483-4081. 2432 Chelsea, Kansas City, MO 64127.

Porter Wagoner is a veritable icon in the country music industry. He is widely acknowledged by new country performers as the epitome of showmanship. His career was launched in 1955 and just two years later, in 1957, he was invited to join the Grand Ole Opry. He started the syndicated "Porter Wagoner Show" in 1960 and it remained on the air for twenty-one years. Porter has a big presence on TNN as one of the regular hosts of *Opry Backstage* on Saturday nights.

Billy Walker is an Opry legend who was born in Ralls, Texas, and was one of eight children. At the age of fifteen, he gave his heart to the Lord. "If God does not guide your life, regardless of your field of endeavor, success is shallow. We are to let our lights shine to all the world. My desire is that God be glorified in *everything* I do."

Lari White began performing as a child with her brother and sister as the White Family Singers. She went to Miami University on a full academic scholarship majoring in music engineering, before winning first place on TNN's *You Can Be A Star* show in 1988. She signed to RCA Records in 1992 and has charted several hits from her four albums. Married to songwriter Chuck Cannon she now has a new baby and a new label. She is the first artist on Disney's fledgling record label, Lyric Street. Her new single and album entitled *Stepping Stones* will be in stores this July.

John and Audrey Wiggins are brother and sister from the Smoky Mountains of North Carolina. They've been performing together for last nineteen years. In January of 1987, they moved to Nashville, Tennessee, to pursue their love of music. After many ups and downs, they remain in Nashville writing and performing, finally living out their dream.

Permissions

The Chain of Love. Reprinted by permission of Jonnie Barnett, Broadmoor Music (BMI) and Balmur Entertainment, Inc./Pugwash Music (BMI), and Rory Lee and Melanie Howard Music, Inc. (ASCAP). ©1998 Jonnie Barnett and Rory Lee.

A Special Gift. Reprinted by permission of Marijoyce Porcelli. ©1998 Marijoyce Porcelli.

The Trophy. Reprinted by permission of Billy Walker. ©1998 Billy Walker.

Ole Charley. Reprinted by permission of Joe Pritchard. ©1998 Joe Pritchard.

They're Waving at Me. Reprinted by permission of Robert Crum. ©1992 Robert Crum. This story originally appeared in *The Christian Science Monitor.*

The Farm Horse That Became a Champion. Reprinted by permission of Philip B. Kunhardt Jr. ©1959 Philip B. Kunhardt Jr.

Great Love. Reprinted by permission of Michael Peterson. ©1998 Michael Peterson.

Simpler Times. Reprinted by permission of Charles D. Williams, M.D. © 1998 Charles D. Williams, M.D.

Introduction to *A Christmas Guest.* Reprinted by permission of Fred Foster. ©1998 Fred Foster.

A Christmas Guest. Reprinted by permission of Loray El Marlee Publishing.

Momma's Christmas Magic. Reprinted by permission of Nova MacIsaac. ©1998 Nova MacIsaac.

The Right Spirit and *Bird Heaven.* Reprinted by permission of Merilyn Gilliam. ©1998 Merilyn Gilliam.

The Chain. Reprinted by permission of Gary Chapman. ©1998 Gary Chapman.

Teddy Bear. Written by Dale Royal, Tommy Hill, Red Sovine and J. William Denny. Copyright ©1976 Cedarwood Publishing. Used By Permission. All Rights Reserved.

Teddy Bear's Last Ride. Written by Dale Royal and J. William Denny. Copyright ©1976 Cedarwood Publishing. Used By Permission. All Rights Reserved.

I Meant to Do That. Reprinted by permission of Paul Brandt. ©1998 Paul Brandt.

Raymond. Written by Phil Thomas and Luke Reed. Copyright ©1995 Songs of PolyGram International, Inc., and Feels Hunny Hole Music, and Golden Hook Music, a division of RS Entertainment, Inc. (BMI), and Songs of PolyGram International, Inc./Partner Music (BMI). Used By Permission. All Rights Reserved.

Daddy's Little Girl. Reprinted by permission of Kippi Brannon. ©1998 Kippi Brannon.

Just a Plain Ol' Country Girl. Reprinted with permission from *Guideposts* magazine. Copyright ©1977 by *Guideposts,* Carmel, NY 10512.

Confidence Builder. Reprinted by permission of Porter Wagoner. ©1998 Porter Wagoner.

The Dream. Reprinted by permission of John and Audrey Wiggins. ©1998 John and Audrey Wiggins.

The Front-Row Seats. Reprinted by permission of Roxane Russell. ©1997 Roxane Russell.

Dream Big. Reprinted by permission of Rita Batts. © 1998 Rita Batts.

Inspired by Love. Reprinted by permission of Lari White. ©1998 Lari White.

A Cowboy's Last Chance. Reprinted by permission of Dirk Johnson. ©1994 Dirk Johnson.

Big House. Reprinted by permission of Monty Byrom. ©1998 Monty Byrom.

Just Keep Walking. Reprinted by permission of John Jarrard. ©1998 John Jarrard.

The Gift of Dignity. Excerpted from *A Country Music Christmas* by Cathie Pelletier. ©1996 by Cathie Pelletier. Reprinted by permission of Crown Publishers, Inc.

Zell and Fuzz. Reprinted by permission of Peachtree Publishers. ©1998 Peachtree Publishers.

Tyler. Reprinted by permission of Joe Diffie. ©1998 Joe Diffie.

God Bless the U.S.A. From *God Bless the U.S.A.* by Lee Greenwood and Gwen McLin. ©1993 by Lee Greenwood and Gwen McLin. Used by permission of the publisher, Pelican Publishing Company, Inc. and MCA Music Publishing.

God Bless the U.S.A. Words and Music by Lee Greenwood. Copyright ©1984 by Music Corporation of America, Inc. and Songs of PolyGram International, Inc. All Rights Controlled and Administered by Music Corporation of America, Inc. International Copyright Secured. Used By Permission. All Rights Reserved.

Living in a Moment. Reprinted by permission of Ty Herndon. ©1998 Ty Herndon.

Ballerina on a Pink Horse. Reprinted by permission of Barry Ettenger. ©1998 Barry Ettenger.

Achy Breaky Heart. Reprinted by permission of Bruce Burch. ©1996 Bruce Burch.

It's Not the End of the World. Reprinted by permission of Emilio. ©1998 Emilio.

I Will Always Love You. Reprinted by permission of Dolly Parton. ©1998 Dolly Parton.

Healing Music. Reprinted by permission of Walter Moodie. ©1998 Walter Moodie.